Public Servants Studied in Image and Essay

Dedicated to the Memory of
Frances Elizabeth Comee Goodsell
1898–1983
Loving Mother, Brave Widow,
Inspiring Community Activist

Sara Miller McCune founded SAGE Publishing in 1965 to support the dissemination of usable knowledge and educate a global community. SAGE publishes more than 1000 journals and over 800 new books each year, spanning a wide range of subject areas. Our growing selection of library products includes archives, data, case studies and video. SAGE remains majority owned by our founder and after her lifetime will become owned by a charitable trust that secures the company's continued independence.

Los Angeles | London | New Delhi | Singapore | Washington DC | Melbourne

Public Servants Studied in Image and Essay

A Fanfare for the Common Bureaucrat

Charles T. Goodsell

Virginia Polytechnic Institute and State University

Los Angeles | London | New Delhi
Singapore | Washington DC | Melbourne

FOR INFORMATION:

SAGE Publications, Inc.
2455 Teller Road
Thousand Oaks, California 91320
E-mail: order@sagepub.com

SAGE Publications Ltd.
1 Oliver's Yard
55 City Road
London, EC1Y 1SP
United Kingdom

SAGE Publications India Pvt. Ltd.
B 1/I 1 Mohan Cooperative Industrial Area
Mathura Road, New Delhi 110 044
India

SAGE Publications Asia-Pacific Pte. Ltd.
3 Church Street
#10-04 Samsung Hub
Singapore 049483

Printed in the United States of America

Library of Congress Cataloging-in-Publication Data

Names: Goodsell, Charles T., author.

Title: Public servants studied in image and essay :
a fanfare for the common bureaucrat / Charles
T. Goodsell.

Description: Los Angeles : CQ Press, 2019. | Includes
bibliographical references and index.

Identifiers: LCCN 2018002840 | ISBN 9781483382869
(pbk. : alk. paper)

Subjects: LCSH: Civil service—United States. |
Bureaucracy—United States. | Public administration—
United States.

Classification: LCC JK681 .G66 2019 | DDC
351.73092/2—dc23

LC record available at https://lccn.loc.gov/2018002840

This book is printed on acid-free paper.

Acquisitions Editor: Scott Greenan
Editorial Assistant: Sarah Christensen
Production Editor: Jane Haenel
Copy Editor: Ashley Horne
Typesetter: Hurix Digital
Proofreader: Sarah J. Duffy
Indexer: Charles T. Goodsell
Cover Designer: Alexa Turner
Marketing Manager: Jennifer Jones

18 19 20 21 22 10 9 8 7 6 5 4 3 2 1

CONTENTS

PREFACE

This book is about twelve men and women who work for government in the United States. Unlike most scholarship in the field of public administration, I address the American public service at an *individual* unit of analysis, not collective concepts such as organization, policy area, legal issue or "the bureaucracy" writ large.

As the book's first title indicates, I do this by two means of study. One is the essay, a written text of some 3,000 words for each individual studied. An essay is a relatively short composition with a continuous narrative flow that can be read in one sitting. I am the author of the essays, with preliminary drafts reviewed by all affected parties to correct errors or clarify meaning. Apart from agency documents, most of the material found in the essays is based on 5 to 6 hours of open-ended private interviewing of the person concerned. The content of this conversation was temporarily retained in a voice recorder.

The second means of study is a visible image. Each essay is accompanied by a still photograph of its subject that I took. However, the term's larger meaning refers to a 15- to 20-minute video segment in which I ask questions to which the public servant responds. The recorded interaction is unrehearsed and informal so as to reveal the person's spontaneous manner and thoughts. My intention is that readers read the essay first for background and then observe the video to form their own impressions. Access to this video is via the website at https://us.sagepub.com/en-us/nam/public-servants-studied-in-image-and-essay/book244899.

The twelve interviewed individuals chosen were not known personally by myself but recommended by others. The criterion I asked to be used is simply that they are "outstanding" public servants. Five were nominated by their organizations; another five by professional contacts; and two consisted of former graduate students at Virginia Tech, neither of which I had in class. The sample is small and not random, hence generalizing from it in a statistical manner is not possible; but since the depth of qualitative inquiry is so great, there is much to learn to say the least. As matter of fact, this degree of concentration on the individual has made me rethink the nature of public administration research.

My original intent was to include four interview subjects from each of the three levels of the federal system of government. Unfortunately, I was unable to enlarge the number of federal employees beyond two. The reason is that two more I had already approached stopped communicating with me the moment Trump was elected. I assume the reason was they feared the publicity could hurt their careers. Hence, I filled out my roster with two extra persons from local government, and they turned out to be first rate.

The subjects work in four states and the District of Columbia. Since shooting the videos required lugging around seven pieces of luggage, it was possible only to take field trips by car and not by flying. Limits on the checkout time of the video equipment from Virginia Tech, added to the driving time, required me to stay within nearby states. Each trip involved two days of contact, one devoted to interviewing and the second to video shooting.

Before commencing field research, I submitted the project to my university's Institutional Review Board. It was judged as not being subject to review in that my research is more in the nature of oral history than social science.

From the standpoint of how this project fits in to other literature in the field, many books of administrator biography or leader profiles have been published, but none to my knowledge have examined in detail the work and careers of a set of individual living bureaucrats. For a list of the many treatments of high-level administrative personalities, see the endnote.[1] The closest thing I found to a volume covering concrete details of the lives of lower level government personnel depicts experiences of members of the armed forces via photographs and accompanying commentary. Although also employing both image and essay, that volume's scope and approach are entirely different.[2]

NOTES

1. Arthur W. Macmahon and John D. Millett, *Federal Administrators* (New York: Columbia University Press, 1939). Eugene Lewis, *Public Entrepreneurship* Bloomington: Indiana University Press, 1980). Herbert Kaufman, *The Administrative Behavior of Federal Bureau Chiefs* (Washington, DC: Brookings Institution, 1981). Theodore W. Taylor, ed., *Federal Public Policy* (Mt. Airy, MD: Lemond, 1984). Jameson W. Doig and Erwin C. Hargrove, eds., *Leadership and Innovation* (Baltimore: Johns Hopkins Press, 1987). Erwin C. Hargrove and John C. Glidewell, eds., *Impossible Jobs in Public Management* (Lawrence: University Press of Kansas, 1990). Terry L. Cooper and N. Dale Wright, eds., *Exemplary Public Administrators* (San Francisco: Jossey-Bass, 1992). Norma M. Riccucci, *Unsung Heroes* (Washington, DC: Georgetown University Press, 1995).

2. Matthew Naylons and Lewis J. Korman, *A Day in the Life of the United States Armed Forces* (New York: HarperCollins, 2003).

ACKNOWLEDGMENTS

It goes without saying that I could not have written this book without the cooperation of my subjects and their nominators. My deep appreciation is hereby extended to all of them. As for key individuals who helped in other ways, Charisse Kiino of CQ Press and SAGE encouraged me four years ago to undertake this project when I brought it to her attention. Several of the publisher's editors, named at the front of the book, were indispensable to carrying out and completing the project. My deepest thanks to all of these individuals. I am indebted to Edward Sewell, a retired professor of communications at Virginia Tech, for suggesting that I include videos in the book. Andrew Tweedt of Virginia Tech's Innovation Space unit patiently converted my raw video feed to usable digital formats each time I returned from the field. My wife Liz, as usual, endured my travels graciously and acted as my indispensable spelling expert each time I was stumped.

INTRODUCTORY REMARKS

In almost all cases, writers on public administration look at public servants from the outside. This perspective ignores what's on the inside. By "inside" I mean their inner drives, sensibilities, and feelings. What we typically do as scholars is assess, from *our* vantage point, conduct as observed and attitudes as assumed. The gathered evidence, then, is quantified, categorized, and tabulated as variables, trends, or probabilities. This "empirical" work is then modeled so we can seek causes and postulate consequences.

The literature is full of examples. Most of them have a negative valance in view of general suspicions about the motives and failings of our bureaucrats as a class. I offer some concluding generalizations from such work:

- Bureaucrats have rule-obsessed personalities.

- Those at the street level bend the rules for their own purposes.

- Public employees do not work hard without incentives.

- Bureaucrats vote Democratic to retain big government.

- They are dehumanized by working in an inhuman bureaucracy.

- They are fear-driven by oppressive hierarchical controls.

- Agents cannot be trusted to obey the instructions of principals.

- Public service motivation can be boiled down to four variables.

I think we can do better. Instead of jumping to premature generalizations, we can do more exploration at the baseline unit of analysis (i.e., the individual public servant). It is time for at least some of us to shift our ontological position from studying bureaucrats as external objects. Yes, we scholars are inevitably outsiders and are stuck with that status. However, efforts can be made mentally and behaviorally to shift as far as possible to another paradigm and see bureaucrats as more than "data." This means making an honest effort to see them as unique, separate persons who dwell in their own life-world of work, career, and personal destiny. We should try to enter that world on a vicarious basis. As fellow human beings, we owe them that. Any beautiful woman can tell you what it's like to be studied as an object.

This will help us move from away the selfish point of view of scholars who are trying to understand a governed society. How can we write good articles about police officers, for example, if we do not know what a state trooper feels like when working a bloody, fatal highway crash? Once I rode along with an officer, and as we made our way down the interstate, he pointed out exactly where this and that happened and how many people were slaughtered.

And we owe it to the public servants themselves to find out more about their inner worlds. By showing them you care about how they think about their work life, you validate the pride they show to their children and colleagues. We may alert them to issues they need to think about more. Repeated encounters with in-depth researchers could accumulate into new degrees of self-realization. This, then, strengthens their determination to expand their quota of added contribution to the public weal.

I have yet another reason to promote this kind of study, that is, to achieve a lasting record of experiences and stories told by public servants over time. In classroom work or available publications, this material can give impetus to interest on the part of the new generation to consider public service as a career. Going into government is not just a way to get by in the short run or to have health benefits but is an opportunity to dedicate one's life to giving as well as taking.

Thus, I have written a book that attempts to get inside the minds of twelve public servants. To carry out this project, I realized early on that I must earn the unwavering trust of my subjects if I were to succeed. I promised them that audio recordings of our private conversations would be destroyed after they served their purpose. They were informed that whatever I wrote about them would be subject to their approval before going into print. I refused the publisher's request to prepare study questions on each essay, since that would give voice to sentiments about them from an external perspective rather than on their own terms.

To be able to make these promises, however, I needed to select interviewees who had favorable reputations to start with. This was necessary so that I could write about them honestly without endangering their future careers by mentioning bad moments. The methodologists will immediately point out that I am cherry picking and not using a random sample that allows one to generalize. My answer is that depth of understanding in scholarship must sometimes trump elegant conclusions. Moreover, learning about outstanding bureaucrats in action rather than mediocre ones will more likely inspire readers seeking direction in their own careers.

To be confronted by this world made me initially feel lost. But when the relationship is formed by talking for hours, conferring on timing and plans, making a tour of the facilities, driving around to work locations, visiting with colleagues, having lunch in a restaurant, making the voice recorder work, and e-mailing about the still photo and essay text, one realizes that this microcosm of two persons communicating repeatedly becomes its own reality. This reality is then supplemented by interviewing the subject before the video camera so that you, the reader, can arrive at your own interpretation of what is real.

What emerges is a set of fresh new arenas of public action that our textbooks and scholarly literature usually ignore: complex mixes of dreams and disappointment, dynamic processes of change, interaction with other personalities and organizations, and, most beautiful of all, human minds imbued with devotion to a cause, yet utterly realistic about achieving it. We are, in my own opinion, entering through public administration's most fascinating portal of knowledge.

Before concluding this introduction, I would like to say a few words about the book's subtitle. It was inspired by the orchestral composition *Fanfare for the Common Man* by the American composer Aaron Copland (1900–1990). In 1942, shortly after the United States entered World War II, the director of the Cincinnati Symphony, Eugene Goossens, asked Copland to compose a "fanfare" to stir public passions on behalf of the men volunteering for military service and the women accepting work in war plants. After much thought, Copland decided to make the target of his fanfare "the common man," a phrase inspired by a speech by then Vice President Henry A. Wallace titled the "Century of the Common Man." Wallace was known for his leftist political views, and since Copland himself had socialist leanings, the term's proletarian ring attracted him. The Cincinnati Symphony premiered the two-minute piece not as a socialist gesture, however, but as a public statement of affirmation for those fighting for the nation's survival.[1]

It occurred to me when planning this book that the phrase "common man" can also apply to public servants (if "man" is used in the generic mankind sense). In America, at least, bureaucrats are not members of a remote elite but are "commoners," living ordinary lives all over the country. Moreover, they harbor values and opinions largely matching those of the general public. In our rhetoric, we charge public servants with seeking "the common good."

At our present moment in history, I would like to adopt the logic of Maestro Goossens in that, just as 1942 was a dark time for the United States, our present time is dark as well. Because of bitter divisions rending the nation's social fabric and gross incompetence plaguing the presidency, we need to sound a fanfare of faith that our "common bureaucrat" professionals will help take us through this ordeal.

For online video interviews of subjects, see https://us.sagepub.com/en-us/nam/public-servants-studied-in-image-and-essay/book244899

NOTE

1. Wikipedia article on Copland, retrieved February 20, 2014. See also Elizabeth B. Grist, *Music for the Common Man: Aaron Copland during the Depression and War* (Oxford: Oxford University Press, 2005).

PART ONE

PUBLIC SAFETY

ADAM R. PRICE, ATF Special Agent

A Firearms Agency under Fire

Photo by Charles T. Goodsell

A lmost all Americans know that the initials "FBI" stand for the Federal Bureau of Investigation, but not everyone knows what "ATF" stands for. Literally, this acronym stands for Alcohol, Tobacco, and Firearms, a shortened form for the Bureau of Alcohol, Tobacco, Firearms, and Explosives. This Bureau is a much smaller federal law enforcement agency than the FBI, acting alongside it in the Department of Justice and just as competently. However, unlike the FBI, it is surrounded by chronic political controversy—it is much admired by law enforcement professionals but hated by the National Rifle Association.

The formation of ATF can be traced to the beginnings of the republic when, in January 1791, Congress passed the first national internal revenue excise tax, called the Distilled Spirits Tax Act. This tax was levied after the newly formed federal government agreed to assume the Revolutionary War debts of the original thirteen states. Congress imposed taxes on both domestic and imported distilled spirits, and fourteen revenue districts were established, with a revenue supervisor, inspector of the survey, and revenue collectors assigned to each. The tax proved so unpopular with the citizenry that in 1794 the Whiskey Rebellion broke out. As the government moved in to arrest the rioting mobs, a revenue officer was killed, perhaps the first on-duty death of a federal agent in the new republic.

After the Volstead Act was passed in 1919, a Prohibition Unit was established within the Bureau of Internal Revenue, the second precursor to the ATF. Bootleggers, gangs, and corrupt politicians formed an underground alliance to oppose this unit's mission and gained great power, most notably in Chicago. A special agent by the name of Eliot Ness took on the task of confronting the Chicago mob, and eventually his team sent the famous criminal Al Capone to jail. Ness's exploits inspired the creation of the comic strip figure Dick Tracy and, much later, the film *The Untouchables*.

When the Prohibition Unit's mission evaporated with the repeal of Prohibition in 1933, the organization was converted into the Alcohol Tax Unit within the Internal Revenue Service, tasked with collecting federal excise taxes on the newly legal sale of liquor. Then, in 1951, collection of federal taxes was extended to tobacco as well.

In 1968, a sea change occurred when Congress passed the Gun Control Act in the wake of the assassinations of John F. Kennedy, Malcolm X, Martin Luther King, and Robert Kennedy. This act remains the organic federal firearm statute on the books. The early revenue function meant that the agency was to remain with the Treasury Department until 1972—considered the birth year of the modern ATF—when a Bureau of Alcohol, Tobacco, and Firearms was created with independent agency status.

Meanwhile, another relevant new law had become effective, the Explosives Control Act of 1970. It defined possession of an unregistered explosive device as a firearm crime, thereby falling under ATF jurisdiction. Two decades later, the bombings of the World Trade Center and the Oklahoma City Federal Building, followed nearly a decade later by the attacks of 9/11, augmented the importance of explosives as weapons of domestic terrorism. The overall importance of ATF's mission was elevated, and Congress added the word "Explosives" to the agency's name after passage of the Homeland Security Act of 2002. This same legislation transferred ATF from the Treasury Department to the Department of Justice, where it now resides.[1]

Our study subject, Adam R. Price, was born into the family of a Kentucky state trooper named Philip Price. At the time, the Prices lived in the small town of Prestonsburg along the Levisa Fork of the Big Sandy River. Because Adam's father was frequently transferred from one state police post to another around eastern Kentucky, the young man experienced the state's entire Appalachian mountain territory. Given the area's ubiquitous moonshine stills, Philip Price became actively engaged with combating them. By the time son Adam began school, his father had resigned from the state police to join the U.S. Treasury's Alcohol and Tobacco Tax Unit as a special investigator. In this job, Philip had his hands full pursuing untaxed liquor violations and breaking up bootleg gangs, exploits that made a deep impression on his son. For the next two decades, the first Special Agent Price remained steadfastly committed to a full career of public service and remained in what became ATF until his retirement in 1988.

It is not surprising, then, that Adam Price inherited an ethos of public service in law enforcement. Not only was his father a model in this regard, but family stories spoke of his grandfather's career as a policeman. Not surprisingly, when Adam went off to college at Michigan State University, he majored in criminal justice. Upon graduating, he headed from the campus fifty miles east to Detroit, where he became a uniformed sworn police officer in the urban community of Clawson, Michigan. Located near major arteries to and from Detroit, the job provided the newly minted policeman with plenty of assault, drug, and robbery cases. He became, in his own words, a "24/7/365" cop who could not wait for his shift to begin, loved being at the center of action, and who, along with his fellow police officers, ran toward gunfire rather than from it. Even though he realized that, with his badge and gun, he was looked upon by many residents with suspicion, fear, and even hatred, he could also in this circumstance help young people in trouble, protect the innocent from criminals, and prevent crime where possible. Looking back, Adam says this was "the best job I ever had."

After three years in the Clawson department, Adam accepted a patrolman job in Arlington County, Virginia. This position put him in the Washington, D.C., area, not far from the ATF national headquarters building at 650 Massachusetts Avenue N.W. At the time, his father was still employed by that agency, and as it turned out, only a year from retirement. The lure of following in his father's footsteps by doing law enforcement on a national level was irresistible. ATF was, after all, tops in the field of violent crime enforcement in that it pursued the worst types of armed felons, bombers, and arsonists. Following one year with the Arlington force, Adam applied for and obtained a slot at ATF, and the second-generation Special Agent Price began a 28-year career in the ATF.

Agent Price's first assignment was to the Miami field office as a criminal investigator, a role similar to that of a detective in a big city police department. As such, he wore civilian clothes but carried the ATF badge and handgun. Prior to being placed on duty, he was sent to the Federal Law Enforcement Training Center in Brunswick, Georgia, to undergo 16 weeks of rigorous preparation, a period longer than that required of most state and local officers at that time. Upon completion of a training program covering criminal/constitutional law, criminal investigative procedures, ethics, nonlethal force, and techniques of firearm, bomb, and arson investigations, he was admitted to the special-agent cadre of the ATF. These officers constitute ATF's arm for locating and apprehending violent breakers of the law. They are distinct from a force of ATF Industry Operations Investigators (IOIs), who monitor legitimate alcohol, tobacco, firearms and explosive activities. As such, they do things such as inspect manufacturing plants and regulate dealer sales. Even though unarmed and without law enforcement powers, IOIs serve a vital function in criminal investigations and weapons trafficking.

Special Agent Price's work at the Miami field office was multifaceted in both geographic and operational terms. In addition to Miami-Dade County, his jurisdiction ranged in practice over much of South Florida, including down to Key West. Because Miami is a hub of international shipping and air travel to the Caribbean and Latin America, his job required him to become active in national and transnational task forces responsible for investigating arms and narcotics trafficking in those regions. An example of his work is his successful investigation and prosecution of a South Florida man who had illegally acquired and trafficked hundreds of assault weapons to Trinidad and Tobago, where they were used in a coup d'état that devastated the island nation for years afterward.

Although Adam often worked with other agents on IOI teams, ATF also encouraged its agents to independently conduct investigations, giving him the professional latitude and discretion he had enjoyed as a police officer. He personally conducted surveillance operations, tapped phones, staffed stakeouts, recruited informants, went undercover, and chased and arrested suspects, often at gunpoint. At the culmination of every investigation, he was expected to take sufficiently convincing evidence to a prosecutor for a federal criminal trial, conviction, and sentencing.

To help with the latter, Adam developed personal ties with several prosecutors who specialized in firearms cases in the South Florida U.S. attorney's office. He also cultivated acquaintanceships in the local police departments in that part of the state, in the region's state police posts, and in other federal field offices in the area, such as the FBI and Drug Enforcement Administration (DEA). A lesson he never forgot is how critical it is for a successful cop at any level to build and maintain a personal network of key people and resources across all jurisdictions and occupations.

Putting dangerous criminals behind bars requires not merely street smarts but a ready command of criminal law. When I talked with Adam about the legal tools essential for an ATF agent, he recited chapter and verse from the Gun Control

Act of 1968, particularly the Armed Career Criminal Act of 1984 amendments. A significant part of Adam's investigative time in South Florida was spent enforcing this law. Title 18 USC Section 924e contains a "three strikes you're out" provision whereby persons previously convicted of three or more crimes of violence, and who are subsequently arrested while in possession of a firearm, must be automatically sentenced to at least 15 years in prison with no opportunity for early release. This statute targeted the "worst of the worst" most violent and active criminals, removing them from the community with lengthy federal prison sentences. Section 924c, a separate sentencing enhancement tool, states that, if a firearm is carried during and in relation to a drug trafficking crime or a crime of violence, varied sentence extensions can be imposed depending on the seriousness of gun use (i.e., 5 years for possession, 7 for brandishing, 10 for discharging, and 30 for machine gun or silencer deployment). No less than 78 percent of all ATF cases involve firearms.

This concentration on gun-related crimes has led the Bureau to specialize in the science and art of what is called gun tracing. This term refers to the identification of the history of a particular firearm from manufacture to the point of first retail sale and beyond. Obviously, this matter is of seminal importance in apprehending and convicting shooters; hence, it is not illogical that ATF is the only organization in the country that does it. In Martinsburg, West Virginia, the agency maintains the National Tracing Center (NTC). In its building are stacked thousands of boxes stuffed with millions of yellow *4473* forms filled out by gun dealers and gun purchasers at the original point of sale. This antiquated system of paper purchase records has not been computerized because the National Rifle Association has convinced Congress it would represent an ominous step toward government registration and eventual seizure of all private firearms.

The tracing process begins when a police department or similar agency submits to the NTC the make, model, and serial number of a firearm found at the scene of a crime. Next, calls are made to the gun's manufacturer and wholesale distributor in order to run down the selling retailer. Once the original buyer has been ascertained, that person is contacted to determine whether the weapon has been passed on to others. If so, investigations are conducted to locate and interview the current owner/possessor. Because of the paper-record requirement, the process may take as little as a few hours in an urgent case; however, on average, it takes some 10 days—a delay that can easily jeopardize solving a crime.

After 10 years as an ATF special agent in Miami, Adam was promoted from street-level criminal investigation to a series of supervisory and middle-management positions. His first assignment was at the Louisville Field Division, whose jurisdiction covered his home state of Kentucky as well as Indiana, West Virginia, and Ohio. The new job was that of senior operations officer, whose responsibility is to monitor the quality and adequacy of investigations conducted by currently practicing agents. After digesting case files and investigative reports, Adam would make a point of personally contacting agents whose case files suggested that errors or other shortcomings had occurred and arrange for corrections to be made before the reports were finalized at the division level. He said he did this most often without notifying his division leadership; having been there himself, he was well aware of the difficulties faced by a cop making fast decisions under the most trying circumstances. He did not want to see the efforts of hard-working street agents slowed by administrative paperwork issues.

Three years later, Special Agent Price was transferred to agency headquarters in Washington, bringing him back to the physical environs of his year in Arlington. Initially attached as staff aide to a Bureau deputy assistant director, he drafted policy memoranda, rewrote outdated directives, and prepared letters to members of Congress in response to constituent complaints. This experience deepened his understanding of the agency's policymaking processes and its many political challenges.

policy

Following this assignment, our subject was moved to the headquarters branch of Advanced Investigations, where as a program manager, and later branch chief, he designed and delivered training programs to enhance the professional competence of new and existing agents. Topics included domestic and international firearms trafficking, undercover operations, cognitive interviewing, money laundering, alcohol and tobacco tax diversion, and crime intelligence analysis. On the basis of his experience in Miami and elsewhere, Adam became recognized as an expert in international firearms trafficking and spoke on that subject to law enforcement audiences from Canada, Mexico, and Europe, as well as around the United States.

training

The next four years of Adam's career were spent once again in the field, this time at the ATF division office in Phoenix, whose jurisdiction covered Arizona, New Mexico, Colorado, Wyoming, and Utah. Initially, he directed the division's Intelligence Operations Group, a unit that supervised information-gathering activities, analysis, and assets in the five states of the Phoenix division's area of responsibility. Later, when he was serving as acting assistant special-agent-in-charge, a group of Tucson-based agents conceived of an enforcement operation they named Wide Receiver. According to the plan, gun shop owners in the area were to be asked to contact the Phoenix division whenever a large and likely illegal gun buy was in progress, especially if it included the AK-47s popular with Mexican drug cartels. The plan was to instruct the shop owner to go ahead with the sale after a surveillance team was put in place to physically follow the buyer's subsequent movements. Special Agent Price approved trying out the scheme only under the strict provision that Mexican authorities and ATF personnel assigned to Mexico City were informed and involved in advance. Also, the Mexican officials had to agree *in writing* to assume responsibility for the weapons once they had crossed the border and to follow them to their destination. His reasoning was that public safety was more important than making a case and that this chain of surveillance allowed for maximum control of the firearms at all times while still permitting the agents and their Mexican counterparts to develop their investigation. Wide Receiver netted some convictions, but they were of relatively small fish since major cartel figures never crossed the border. Thus, the operation was soon discontinued.

willing to try out new ideas

After Adam left the Phoenix division, an agent there proposed a more sweeping illegal weapon sales operation, patterned in a general way after Wide Receiver but that would presumably catch big fish as well as small ones. However, the plan left the earlier campaign's restrictions behind in two respects: (1) the guns would be allowed to migrate across the border without physical surveillance and (2) the operation would be carried out without informing the Mexican police or the ATF Mexico City office. Called Fast and Furious, the proposal was sent up the ATF hierarchy, discussed at length, and approved by top law enforcement leaders at the Department of Justice. Over a period of 18 months, thousands of powerful assault weapons headed freely south into Mexico. In the absence of any tracking, they disappeared indiscriminately into the Mexican underworld. Alarmed, agents in the Phoenix office warned their superiors that the guns could fall into any hands and be used for mayhem of any kind. In addition to costing innocent lives, they asserted, the operation could jeopardize relations with an important foreign neighbor, put lives at risk on both sides of the border, and still yield zero arrests. But Washington repeatedly refused to halt the program. After a popular U.S. Border Patrol agent was suddenly shot to death by an AK-47 linked to Fast and Furious, the dissenting agents took matters into their own hands and leaked the incident to Senator Charles Grassley, chair of the Senate Judiciary Committee. He immediately went public with it, setting off a media storm that eventually generated a series of congressional hearings hostile to the Bureau. Throughout the scandal, the leadership at the Department of Justice remained quiet about their involvement, allowing all the blame to fall on ATF.[2]

The final active-duty years of Special Agent Price at ATF were spent back at its Washington headquarters. By now, the offices had been moved from the former fashionable Massachusetts Avenue address to a newly constructed building at 99 New York Avenue Northeast, a neighborhood undergoing much-needed rehabilitation. Within these pretentious quarters in an unpretentious part of town, Adam's role in the agency shifted from being a "common bureaucrat" in the sense of this book to that of a top policy adviser to the administration and a trusted representative of his country abroad.

The central theme of this latter portion of Adam's career was to add to the insights of policymakers from his hands-on experience with drug and firearms trafficking across the U.S. southern border. During three years in the agency's Counterterrorism Division, among other tasks he performed was to be ATF's prime liaison to the Department of Homeland Security (DHS). On more than one occasion, he briefed Secretary Janet Napolitano and other DHS officials, along with other members of the intelligence community, on the possibilities for terrorist access to weapons and explosives due to vulnerabilities in U.S. firearms and explosives laws. In 2010, he was shifted from that job to the Firearms Operations Division to help deal with the political uproar following the surfacing of Fast and Furious; this involved aid in preparing a response by the agency to a critical Government Accountability Office report on it. In addition, Adam worked with Bureau leadership, drafting new internal controls that would shape future investigations, in particular ones that would prevent the recurrence of similar incidents and follow new procedures.

Then in 2012, Adam returned to the Counterterrorism Division at an even more senior advisory role. He regularly engaged in discussions with officials at the DHS, Central Intelligence Agency, Office of National Drug Control Policy, and National Security Council on the implications of gun trafficking across the southern border for combating terrorism and organized crime. The assignment also included authoring the weapons chapter for the president's *2013 National Southwest Counter-Narcotics Strategy*, a key government-wide planning document.

At this time, Special Agent Price also found himself serving in a quasi-diplomatic role in Mexico City. He went there frequently to consult with Mexican officials on border crime. A major piece of his charge was to represent the views of the U.S. government in preparing a draft bilateral agreement between the two governments that would incorporate a greater understanding of the dynamics and implications of illegal gun trafficking southward into Mexico. In these deliberations, Adam had to find a balance between Mexico's goal of stamping out such weapons while simultaneously pointing out to the Mexican representatives the rights guaranteed to all Americans under the Second Amendment. This included explaining the peculiarly divisive politics in America surrounding gun control.

This fact of political life in the United States arises, of course, from the struggle between those outraged by mass shootings and groups like the National Rifle Association (NRA). The fallout from this fight has done much to create a hostile political environment for ATF. Although the agency has solid friends in many places—for example, local law enforcement officers around the country—that support is relatively silent compared to the loud opposition received from pro-gun quarters.

Several attempts have been made to dissolve ATF or hand its duties over to other agencies. While campaigning for the presidency, Ronald Reagan wooed support from NRA members by pledging to abolish it. The NRA sought to whip up public support for the move by producing a television documentary in which Congressman John Dingell of Michigan (an NRA board member) described ATF agents as "a jackbooted group of fascists." Upon taking office, Reagan announced plans to make good on his pledge, but because of opposition from other federal law enforcement agencies, police fraternal organizations, as well as fire departments and state fire marshals who relied on ATF's resources and expertise to combat arson crimes, he later retreated to proposing it be transferred into the Secret Service. ATF agents actually liked that notion, but the NRA suddenly realized that this would enhance the agency's prestige, making the agency politically difficult to impede and control. Hence, they lobbied against the measure, killing it.[3]

In 1993, the NRA tried again to abolish the agency, but the Clinton administration was not receptive. In 2006, Representative James Sensenbrenner (R-Wisconsin), recipient of an NRA "Defender of Freedom" award, struck pay dirt by using reauthorization of the Patriot Act as a vehicle for requiring Senate confirmation of the ATF director. This step has opened the door to political manipulation in that official's selection. Meanwhile, at the lofty but vaporous cultural level of urban legend, rumors are continuously circulating within the right-wing underground that ATF is planning "to take away our guns" as part of a secret conspiracy to strip Americans of their Second Amendment rights. In January 2017, Sensenbrenner reintroduced a previously proposed bill titled the ATF Elimination Act, which would see ATF dissolved, with its criminal enforcement functions transferred to the FBI and regulatory functions transferred to the DEA. It did not pass.

A consensus exists among many in the ATF world that, because of NRA influence, the amount of resources allocated by Congress to the Bureau have been kept minimal over its history, to the extent that it cannot effectively carry out its mandate of suppressing firearms-related violent crime in America as the U.S. population grows. A "Hidden Life of Guns" investigation by the *Washington Post* in 2010 reported that the level of roughly 2,500 on-duty ATF agents has not materially changed since the agency's creation in 1972. Over the same 38 years, it was pointed out that the number of agents fielded by the U.S. Marshal Service increased from 1,900 to 3,300, by the DEA from 1,500 to 5,000, and by the FBI from 8,700 to 13,000.[4] Detailed employee data furnished by ATF itself confirms a near-static condition. Between Fiscal Years 2001 and 2013, the number of ATF agents varied within the narrow band of 2,317 in 2001 to 2,562 in 2010. Then, over three years following 2010, the number of agents declined to 2013's figure of 2,402. A parallel three-year slow decline occurred as well in total employment and amount of budgeted funds.[5]

How, then, does Special Agent Price feel about spending a career of 28 years in the poorly funded Bureau of Alcohol, Tobacco, Firearms, and Explosives? When I asked him that question, he said that if he had the chance to do it all over again he would take exactly the same path. Because the agency's mission is defined in terms of the illegal use of firearms and explosives—the key operant feature of the worst and most dangerous criminal acts—it provides a wide range of deeply important and action-filled opportunities for law enforcement service. Adam has experienced large-scale international investigations in Miami, the satisfaction of tutoring other agents in the craft of smart policing, the chance to guide a well-conceived firearms-tracking operation that operated without mishap, positions in which he can shape agency policy, the opportunity to lecture before law enforcement professionals from abroad, the privilege of advising officials in high places such as the White House situation room, as well as the rare experience of conducting sensitive negotiations between two countries.

Since his retirement, Adam continues to remain actively engaged in the important work of public safety and violence prevention. He serves as a consultant to government and academia in the matters of law enforcement, intelligence, and international affairs. Adam also acts as a consultant to the United Nations, providing advice and training to international audiences in the areas of small arms and light weapons nonproliferation, police capacity building, and establishing the rule of law in post-conflict zones.

It is Adam's conviction that a career in public safety is intense, dangerous, and often frustrating but is also tremendously satisfying when you know you've removed a violent predator or firearms trafficker from the streets and saved innocent lives by doing so. Over his career, he has been able to live this passion in scores of ways, thereby honoring his family legacy and agency legacy to the fullest. Moreover, he has never considered jumping ship for an agency enduring less political controversy and profiting from more resources. This steadfast loyalty to his organization not only sets a high standard for the common bureaucrat but has led him to the top of his profession, where he has become a national and international resource.

NOTES

1. Bureau of Alcohol, Tobacco, Firearms and Explosives, "Our History" and "Eliot Ness," retrieved online January 27, 2018.

2. William J. Vizzard, *In the Cross Fire: A Political History of the Bureau of Alcohol, Tobacco and Firearms* (Boulder, CO: Lynne Rienner, 1997), 1–4, 17, 40–43, 94.

3. For added details see Charles T. Goodsell, *The New Case for Bureaucracy* (Thousand Oaks: CQ Press, 2015), 173–175.

4. Erik Larson, *Lethal Passage: The Story of a Gun* (New York: Vintage Books, 1995), 140–142.

5. Sari Horwitz and James V. Grimaldi, "Firearms Watchdog on Short Leash," *Washington Post*, October 26, 2010.

MICHAEL J. BENDER, Police Captain

Cops Doing Mental Health

Photo by Charles T. Goodsell

The scene of this public safety essay is Richmond, Virginia, the capital of the state. It is a city of 220,000 within a metro area of 1.3 million. In American history, this place was where the revolutionary Patrick Henry shouted, "Give me liberty or give me death." Seventy years later, it was the center of another revolution, the secessionist Confederacy presided over by Jefferson Davis. The historic capitol building still in use but much since expanded was designed by Thomas Jefferson.

Richmond's original police department was established in 1807, making it one of the earliest formally organized municipal law enforcement agencies in the country. During the Civil War, its officers were absorbed into the Virginia state militia. At the war's end, the function of policing was taken over by the Union's military government. In 1870, President Grant readmitted Virginia into the United States, at which time the current police department was founded.

At present, the Richmond Police Department consists of approximately 700 sworn officers and 125 civilian employees. It operates on a budget in the neighborhood of $86 million. Of the officers, 62 percent are white, 25 percent black, and 16 percent female. Despite these proportions, many top leadership posts are filled by African Americans and women. A goal of the department is that each group of new recruits consists of at least 20 percent women and 40 percent persons of color.

Organizationally, the department's law enforcement activities are divided among four precincts. Each is under the command of a captain, with an executive officer in charge of daily management. First Precinct covers the less affluent east side. Second Precinct serves the population south of the James River that courses through the city. Third Precinct extends out to the west, and Fourth Precinct includes downtown plus upscale neighborhoods to the north. All four precincts are divided into three patrol sectors, each led by a lieutenant.

The department's headquarters is located centrally in a large modern building at 200 West Grace Street. From it, an officer at the rank of major oversees Area One, consisting of the first and second precincts, with a second overseer at this rank doing so for Area Two, embracing the third and fourth precincts. Commanding the department as a whole is Chief of Police Alfred Durham, appointed in 2015 following 17 years of leadership in the District of Columbia Police Department.[1]

Michael J. Bender Jr., although not a native of Richmond proper, has lived most of his life in suburbs nearby. His father was a career officer in the U.S. Army. Upon retirement from the military, Michael Sr. became a Virginia state employee and eventually headed operations of a Commonwealth central warehouse. Mike's mother, Nita Williams Bender, is a retired civil servant at the federal level in Washington. Within the Department of Defense, she rose to become chief of the Education Supplies Procurement Office that supplies DoD schools around the world. Inevitably, young Michael as he was growing up heard numerous stories about the tribulations and satisfactions of life within state, federal, and military bureaucracies.

The underlying theme the young man drew from the experiences of his parents was the importance of choosing a career field dedicated to service. In selecting a direction, Mike felt attracted to two possibilities: the military and law enforcement. At the time, however, the military was undergoing funding cutbacks and the chances of being commissioned without attending a military academy seemed slim. Moreover, the relative peacetime then prevailing did not provide the action and adventure for which the young man thirsted. So, by default, he chose law enforcement—an occupation he perceived as filled with unending danger and excitement. When Mike enrolled at Virginia Commonwealth University he selected criminal justice as his major. In 1993, he graduated with a Bachelor of Science degree in administration of justice.

Bender joined the Richmond Police Department in January 1995. His first six months on the job were spent as a member of the 72nd class of recruits at the Richmond Police Academy. This is an in-house, nonresidential police training school on the campus of Virginia Union University. It operates in its own modern building packed with relevant equipment including a state-of-the-art firing range equipped with a 360-degree "Shoot, Don't Shoot" Force Simulator. This apparatus introduced Mike to the dilemma that all police face when, within an instant, they must decide whether to kill or risk being killed. The solemnity of this moment is recognized by recruits when, at the beginning of each training day, they stand silently at attention to salute portraits of the department's fallen officers.

The day after graduation, newly minted Police Officer Michael J. Bender was assigned to nighttime patrol duty in Second Precinct, whose three sectors lie in an industrial and low-income area south of the river. The size of the force then available for this shift consisted of five officers: three veterans and two rookies, one of whom was Michael.

Richmond's south side had long been affected by unemployment and drug gangs. In the mid-1990s, the city generally was one of the most crime-ridden cities in the country with an annual homicide rate around 160, one of the worst in the country for a municipality of this size (the figure is now approximately 40). This meant that Officer Bender was confronted with danger and chaos on a scale he did not anticipate. As he headed alone through the dark streets in his cruiser, Michael frequently came across crimes in progress, such as armed robberies and gang fights. At the same time, his police radio would crackle with dispatcher calls about other assaults, burglaries, domestic violence, and murder. To make matters worse, the calls multiplied on each other; before one could be fully handled another would come through. Soon a third or even fourth would pile on, all before any could be fully resolved. The uppermost imperative amid this turmoil was to be ready to rush elsewhere whenever a fellow officer called for backup.

Yet, with time, Mike learned how to keep cool and cope, allowing his trained skills and seemingly natural aptitude for the job to carry him through. After a few months, the young officer drew notice from his superiors. They began assigning him specialized duties beyond doing routine street patrol. For example, he was given an opportunity to take the policing-by-bicycle course at the academy and then be assigned to patrol downtown sidewalks. This allowed Mike to develop a facility for engaging citizens in casual conversation, an ability that would come in very handy later in his career.

Over the next years, Bender periodically sat for promotion exams with considerable success. In 2001, he advanced to the rank of detective and joined the Robbery Task Force. Two years later, he was promoted to sergeant and transferred to Third Precinct as platoon leader. Another special assignment became available, that of participating in a citywide campaign to attack gang distribution of crack cocaine. With his leadership skills becoming increasingly evident to superiors, Mike was soon instructing newly promoted sergeants at the academy. Then in 2006, greater leadership responsibility came when he was advanced from platoon leader to sector head and sent back to his old Second Precinct.

A major next jump up the ladder occurred in 2010, when Sergeant Bender successfully sat for promotion to lieutenant, the equivalent of moving from enlisted man to officer in the military. He advanced to the position of sector officer in charge, first of Sector 211 and then 212 of Second Precinct.

With increasing administrative responsibilities now coming his way, Mike refined his management skills by earning a Local Government Management certificate at Virginia Tech, Richmond branch. This experience encouraged him to apply for formal graduate work at Virginia Tech, and in 2015, he was awarded a Master of Public Administration degree at Virginia Tech's Center for Public Administration and Policy.

In that same year, Lieutenant Bender ascended to a yet higher position in his organization, that of executive officer of First Precinct, the post he occupied when first interviewed for this book. The scope of this job included management of the daily operations of an entire precinct, in effect making him second in command to its captain. If one counts his bicycle patrol assignment in downtown, Bender had by now rotated through all four precincts of the department.

In November 2017 yet another promotion came along for which he was being considered when interviewed. This was to captain. His assignment at that rank became that of Watch Commander, a key position with respect to the department as a whole. The Office of the Watch Commander sees to it that the department functions well 24 hours a day. The commander on duty during off hours becomes a de facto chief of police at night. During each 12-hour shift, Captain Bender alone makes on-the-spot decisions with respect to all reported crimes or emergencies that occur over the entire city. This is, obviously, a major load to bear; now the rookie who once handled the chaos of Second Precinct at night is amplifying that many times over.

As we wish Captain Bender the very best in his new assignment, it is important to explain why I labeled this essay "Cops Doing Mental Health." It is because, while occupying the field officer positions mentioned above, Michael took it upon himself to undertake the added task of leading the way in reforming how the Richmond Police Department confronts mental health.

For some years, a movement has been afoot in progressive police departments around the country known as Crisis Intervention. It calls for a combination of police and medical actions at the level of the individual citizen. The notion of "crisis" as conceived in the mental health field has been defined as "a brief episode of intense emotional distress in which the person's usual coping efforts are insufficient to handle the challenges confronting the individual."[2] Anyone can experience such episodes, but in those afflicted by personality disorders or outright psychoses such events occur more often and in more serious form.

Mental meltdown episodes that occur privately are normally handled, if at all, by private doctors or clinics. However, those that trigger in public a pattern of bizarre, illegal, and violent acts are likely to be brought to the attention of the police. Hence, the reasoning goes, just as private-practice therapists should know what to do for their patients, first-responder police should act knowledgably with their suspects. If they do not, actions taken in such cases can land the victim in jail when diversion to treatment can in the long term do more to achieve a peaceable society. Justice is served both in the moral sense of avoiding future repetitions of similar behavior and in the practical sense of relieving the overloaded legal system. Furthermore, at this time when minority groups accuse urban police of unnecessarily shooting suspects, sensitive treatment by officers to mentally ill offenders can become one more step in rebuilding community trust.

Concerted thinking on how exactly to do this began following a police shooting scandal that occurred in Memphis in 1988. City officers shot and killed a man who turned out to have a long history of mental illness and substance abuse. Following an eruption of community outrage, a task force was formed of police officers, mental health professionals, and community advocacy groups. The report issued from their deliberations eventually became known as the Memphis Model of CIT (Crisis Intervention Team)—an acronym now standard for appropriate police-based action when mental health is involved.[3]

The core idea of CIT is to utilize ongoing systems of community collaboration to make quick diversion from arrest possible when crisis offenses are minor, followed by appropriate in-depth mental health clinical treatment. When the crime committed is serious and/or violent, arrest and prosecution proceed as usual but with the possibility of mandatory hospital treatment following incarceration or in conjunction with it. Both of these options involve applying the coercive power of the law. The idea of "forgiving" an offender for a violation of law and coercing medical compliance upon a private citizen is defended by the argument that such actions contribute to the long-term safety and well-being of all concerned, including not just the public at large but perpetrators and police as well.

From 2007 to 2009, Michael Bender, then a sergeant in Second Precinct, became interested in the Memphis model. In his capacity of platoon leader, he was aware of calls his officers answered where something more than malicious intent was involved. At the same time, he was a member of the department's Trauma Informed Care Committee, an assignment that brought him into contact with local hospitals.

To bring something like the Memphis model to Richmond obviously required wide collaboration both within and outside the RPD. To move ahead, Bender sought and found two other persons to join him in a small planning group. One of these was Shane Waite, then a patrol officer assigned to the department's homeless task force, also known as HOPE (Homeless Outreach Prevention and Education). This assignment convinced Waite that most homeless men suffer from some form of mental illness or addiction. The second person was Kelly Furgurson, a long-time mental health professional and administrator at the Richmond Behavioral Health Authority (RBHA). This entity serves as Richmond's community service mental health board, one of forty created in Virginia in the wake of mental health care deinstitutionalization several years ago. Like Bender himself, both Waite and Furgurson became deeply involved in the development and operations of Richmond's CIT program. Shane, now a sergeant, serves as its internal CIT coordinator and teaches CIT classes at the academy. Kelly is director of Access Emergency and Medical Services at RBHA and coordinator of the Crisis Triage Center (to be discussed).

This trio of informal founders of Richmond's CIT program fully understood that its success depended upon moving past a mere conceptual model to the point of putting in practice several organizational elements that operate as a single system. The most fundamental of these are (1) a flexible legal framework; (2) a solid police training program; (3) quick ways to detect the presence of mental illness; (4) available clinical capacity for treatment; and (5) arrangements for transporting and holding subjects under continuous control and guard. I comment on each of these components in the remaining pages, in the order they are listed.[4]

With respect to a legal framework, jail diversion efforts in Virginia were first made possible in 2007, when the General Assembly began to approve funding for this purpose.[5] For its part, the Richmond Circuit Court cooperated by creating a special mental health docket for judicial hearings on individual diversion cases. The commonwealth's attorney set into place procedures for review of cases placed on this docket. The local Probation and Parole District of the Virginia Department of Corrections laid the basis for post-treatment monitoring of persons released from custody. Two kinds of statute-based custody orders were made available to authorize mandatory action when subjects refused to cooperate voluntarily: the Emergency Custody Order (ECO), which enables prior psychiatric evaluation, and the Temporary Detention Order (TDO), which authorizes obligatory hospitalization. ECOs are normally issued by the Richmond Behavioral Health Authority and TDOs by city circuit court judges.

The training of officers is done at the Police Academy. The CIT course is 40 hours in length, in accord with accepted standards in the field. Whereas the international minimum standard for training coverage is 25 percent of officers, in Richmond all sworn officers are required to take the course, and if they have not done so, they are not issued Tasers. The training week is also open to outside law enforcement officers, and its reputation has now spread to the point that non-RPD enrollees chronically outnumber those from home.

Officer Bender teaches in the program and is himself an alumnus. Sergeant Waite is on the continuing academy staff and one of its main instructors. Various methodologies of instruction are used. Formal classroom instruction covers mental health issues generally and their tie-in with law enforcement. Individual topics include personality disorders, alcohol and drug abuse, post-traumatic stress, developmental disabilities, common mental health medications, and suicide prevention. Role-plays are used to teach the basic verbal skills required to deescalate crises. Field visits are made to hospitals and other mental health facilities around the city in order to grant familiarity and make contacts.

An essential key to success in CIT is having patrol officers able to detect likely mental problems. This must be done quickly, on the spot. A first recommended step is to see if the suspect can provide a name, address, and identification. A second is to engage the person in casual, open-ended conversation, something like what Michael did from his police bicycle in downtown Richmond. It is important to allow the subject to speak freely as long as needed. The interviewing officer interrupts only to repeat answers to show they are being heard. If appropriate, the officer can ask whether the individual is *having a bad day*, and if so, why. Information is requested on whether he or she is currently under care, and if so, from whom are they receiving care and with what medications. Throughout, officers are told to look for behavioral cues such as crying, stuttering, sweating, and maintaining little eye contact. Incomplete sentences and frequent changes of subject are indicative of unstable thought. A posture of leaning backward or protectively folding arms across the chest may indicate anxiety.[6]

Once a diversion determination is made by the responding officer (with sheer instinct often helping), the relevant officer telephones the crisis dispatcher at the Richmond Behavioral Health Authority (RBHA). Typically, the officer is told to bring the subject to the RBHA building downtown for evaluation under ECO authority, or if mental symptoms are major and dangerous, he or she is taken directly to a hospital. The RBHA maintains a continuously available psychiatric staff to interview subjects, conduct an evaluation, and provide short-term therapy if that is all that is needed. If not, it arranges for a TDO to enable treatment at a cooperating hospital.

Three Richmond area hospitals with psychiatric wards are available, but the one most commonly used for CIT treatment is Chippenham Hospital, located in a western section of the city bearing that name. The two others are Community Hospital and the Medical Center of Virginia Commonwealth University. Chippenham has the largest Psychiatric Department with some 140 beds, and for this reason, Lieutenant Bender and his fellow CIT founders decided from the beginning to make it the medical headquarters for treating most jail-diverted patients.

This hospital is the locale of what is known as the Crisis Triage Center, another name common to CIT programs generally. The word *triage* in this instance does not mean sorting victims by extent of injury, but instead, it refers to the Triage Assessment Model discussed in the mental health literature. This three-dimensional construct posits a trio of separate domains of human mental health to be evaluated: behavioral, cognitive, and affective.[7]

At Chippenham the Triage Center occupies two rooms just inside the locked door to its hospital's Psychiatric wing, just off the front lobby. One space is a small office used by a nurse-receptionist, the other the patient interview room. The latter is furnished with rounded plastic benches bolted to the floor. An observational one-way mirror is on the internal hall side of the interview room and an openable call window in the office connects externally to the lobby. It is in these small chambers that psychiatrists and other mental health professionals interview patients and make weighty decisions on whether hospitalization and temporary detention are necessary. The center is open each day of the week between 2 p.m. and midnight. In addition to Richmond police, officers from several nearby jurisdictions are entitled to use it.

The officers who have taken subjects into custody are responsible—unless otherwise directed—for transporting them securely to the Triage Center and guarding them on its premises until handover. They submit paperwork on their charges through the hallway window. Forms are signed to transfer legal responsibility for retaining custody to police stationed at the hospital itself. Under an arrangement agreed to by all affected parties, the officers that take over are donated by the Richmond Police Department.

The roster for this duty was maintained by Lieutenant Bender in his capacity of police coordinator for the center. When serving on Chippenham duty, RPD officers receive compensation from the department in addition to their normal salary. The department has agreed to accept this personnel cost so its first-responder patrol officers can immediately return to normal duty after handover.

Michael himself voluntarily put in up to 20 hours/ a week on this extra hospital duty, on top of his 40-plus extremely full workweek as executive officer of Second Precinct. This meant that many of his evenings were spent at Chippenham rather than at home. I asked him why he schedules himself such a heavy load in view of the consequences for his personal life. He simply responded that doing service is his life's purpose. That reasoning is now being applied to the extreme as he regularly stays on duty all night as Watch Commander.

NOTES

1. Richmond Police Department, links to Organization, FAQ, Annual Reports, and Chief of Police, retrieved online August 12, 2016, http://www.richmondgov.com/ Police/.

2. Kenneth France, *Crisis Intervention: A Handbook of Immediate Person-to-Person Help*, 4th ed. (Springfield, IL: Charles C Thomas, 2002), 4.

3. Amy C. Watson and Anjali J. Fulambarker, "The Crisis Intervention Team Model of Police Response to Mental Health Crises: A Primer for Mental Health Practitioners," *Best Practices in Mental Health* 8, no. 2 (December 2012): 71–80.

4. Note in this regard, the prime elements mentioned by Randolph Dupont, Sam Cochran, and Sarah Pillsbury, "Crisis Intervention Team Core Elements," University of Memphis Department of Criminal and Criminal Justice, CIT Center, 2007.

5. Office of Forensic Services, Virginia Department of Behavioral Health & Development Services, *Jail Diversion Initiatives: Program Review 2007–2015* (Richmond: Author, 2015), 1.

6. France, *Crisis Intervention*, 32–33.

7. Rick A. Myer, *Assessment for Crisis Intervention: A Triage Assessment Model* (Stamford, CT: Brooks/Cole, 2000), 29–32.

STEPHANIE F. PECHURA, Felon Rehabilitator

Tough Love in Action

Photo by Charles T. Goodsell

O ur third subject in the public safety section of this book does very different work from the previous two. She is not engaged in the crime-stopping side of law enforcement but quite literally the public safety side. Her job is to help make sure that convicted felons of sex crimes who have completed their prison terms are safe to return to society.

Sexual abuse of an adult or child is, of course, a heinous crime. If caught and convicted, the offender is normally sentenced for years in a state penitentiary. Yet, even after the sentence is concluded, the felon may continue to be driven by an urge to commit such crimes. To counter this danger, in 1999, the General Assembly of Virginia passed the Commitment of Sexually Violent Predators Act.[1] It permits the Commonwealth to retain custody of sexual offenders after their sentences are completed as long as they are deemed a serious threat. The state of Washington enacted the first statute of this kind in 1990, and by 2010, twenty states had adopted such a law.

It was not until 2003 that funds were appropriated to implement the 1999 law. In that year, the General Assembly was propelled into action when Paul Martin Andrews, victim of an outrageous sex crime thirty years earlier, publicly protested that the prison term of the perpetrator, Richard Alvin Ausley, was about to end. Ausley had openly boasted in prison that he would do it again when freed.

The crime in question was to kidnap young boys and lock them in a 4 × 4 × 8 plywood box built into the ground in a remote area near Portsmouth, Virginia. Ausley would visit his box daily to assault his captives. Fortunately, Andrews had to endure this torture for only one week. On the seventh day, he heard the box being opened, and it was the police, who had caught on to what was going on. After that incident, Ausley's deeds never resumed, as he was tried, convicted, and committed to a long sentence in prison. As a consequence of his boasting while there, he was murdered by fellow inmates.[2]

To implement the 1999 statute, the Virginia Department of Mental Health, Mental Retardation and Substance Abuse Services was directed to create a new entity, the Virginia Center for Behavioral Rehabilitation (VCBR). For temporary quarters, VCBR was housed in retrofitted residences at Southside Virginia Training Center in Petersburg, Virginia. After the Tim Kaine administration came to office in 2006, the agency was reconceived as a largely independent organization within the Department of Behavioral Health and Development Services.

Meanwhile, a new dedicated facility for VCBR was being built in Burkeville, Virginia, a small town fifty miles southwest of Richmond, on the grounds of Piedmont Geriatric Hospital. By 2008, it was completed at a cost of $62 million. Initially, only a handful of offenders were held there, but over the years, the number rose into the hundreds, in part because the number of covered sexual offenses was expanded from four to twenty-eight. Expansion plans are now being carried out to increase its capacity by half.

Our subject, Stephanie F. Pechura, was born in Milwaukee but spent her youth in Richmond, Virginia, and Bethesda, Maryland. For college, she went west to the

University of Arizona to major in psychology and political science. The first field attracted her attention because since high school she had found herself being asked by chums for advice; interest in the second arose from an internship in Tucson's public defender's office, where she visited clients in jail and worked a case involving a defendant struggling with psychological issues. University courses on the law and mental health cemented the two subject matter areas in her thinking.

After graduating with a bachelor's degree in 1994, Ms. Pechura returned to the east and enrolled in a Master of Social Work (MSW) program at Virginia Commonwealth University in Richmond. The practicum requirements of the program confirmed her sense of career direction. In the first year, she interned as a counselor for teens at the Youth Emergency Shelter and John G. Wood School of the Virginia Home for Boys. In the following summer, a job coordinating a survey of staff morale and public reputations in social service agencies widened her acquaintanceship with the scope of social work institutions. In her second MSW year, experience in adult mental health care in a hospital setting was obtained by an internship at Hunter Holmes McGuire VA Medical Center in Richmond.

After receiving the MSW in 1999, Stephanie was hired as a therapist by a private Richmond agency that rehabilitated juvenile sex offenders. The job provided her first experience with this category of patient. When the organization relocated, she took a therapist position at Central State Hospital in Petersburg, Virginia, joining a team that treated aggressive male mental health patients. In 2002, she was promoted to the position of clinical social work supervisor at Central State, in acknowledgment of her success in enabling long-term patients to undergo the process of being discharged and transitioned into the community.

By this time, the VCBR had been funded, had launched operations in Petersburg, and was looking for staff. Stephanie loved her state hospital job, but this new program offered rare opportunities for creative innovation. It happened that she was one of the very few professionals available with a background in social work, mental health, the custodial environment, and sex offender treatment. They snapped her up, and in 2004, Ms. Pechura became VCBR's first social worker.

Stimulated by the challenge of attempting to rehabilitate adult male sex offenders straight out of prison, she dug into her work and soon discovered that, despite setbacks and the inability to make quick progress, she found it to be rewarding. Here was a chance to turn the lives of human beings headed for nowhere to a path toward a better life.

In 2008, VCBR was relocated in Burkesville. By this time, Stephanie's clinical and leadership talents began to be recognized, and she was promoted to the position of director of Treatment Services for the entire center. This gave her responsibility for supervising scores of master's- and bachelor's-level mental health and behavioral health specialists. Then, in 2010, a major shift from therapy to administration occurred. She was transferred from Treatment Services to the directorship of Program Services. This put her in charge of managing all living units and related service programs.

The position afforded Stephanie a chance to innovate. Instead of feeding the men with a standard tray from a secured distribution station in each living unit, a common cafeteria was created at which the residents themselves helped prepare the day's menu options. Other achievements were setting up a system whereby patients obtained their own self-initiated appointments with doctors or dentists. A vocational training program was added that allows residents to earn certificates for achieving skills that any citizen would need to gain employment.

Then, in 2012, our subject's responsibilities expanded to what they are today, as assistant director of administration. This appointment placed her in a position of responsibility over the management of support services. At this time, the enterprise is sizable, having more than 300 residents, 500 staff, and a budget of $35 million. She works with the Department of Behavioral Health and Developmental Services on the preparation of budgets, development of written policies, and the content of training programs. Special projects add daily spice, such as overseeing necessitated doubled upper-lower bunking, installing a wireless security alarm system, and monitoring the facility's further expansion.

In short, Ms. Pechura is a public administrator in the full, generic sense. In this role, she has adopted a style of being available at all times, including to members of each shift, being in close physical and informational touch with all corners of the organization, remaining ever on the lookout for ways to heighten mission success, and consciously nurturing future leaders to take over. Undergirding her activist approach to management is a sense of legitimacy engendered by years of personal clinical service on the front lines. In retrospect, it seems quite remarkable how Stephanie's experiences in college, graduate school, the private sector, and Central State Hospital accumulated so neatly to prepare her for this work.

The Virginia Center for Behavioral Rehabilitation is an unusual and complex institution. It simultaneously performs two very different functions: the "hard" one of maintaining absolutely secure custody of individuals and, at the same time, the "soft" one of providing them with intensely personal behavioral treatment. It would be easy to imagine how such a drastic mission duality could lead to confused organization schizophrenia or domination by one over the other. My interpretation is, however, that by softening the hard side and hardening the soft one, VCBR's leaders have achieved a reasonably equivalent and quite unified balance between the two. The remainder of this essay is devoted to elaboration of this point.

With respect to the custody subpart, a number of mollifying features can be identified. As for the physical facility itself, it is not one giant multistory structure with barred windows. Apart from a plain front administration building, it consists of four white, nearly cube-shaped single-story buildings interconnected by sealed corridors. The cluster is arranged in a cross, with each arm constituting a main corridor that connects a pair of buildings. The point where the two axes intersect at ninety degrees is called the *knuckle*, a central meeting place for building circulation along hundreds of feet of inner hallway. The corridor walls near the knuckle are covered with giant colorful murals painted by the residents themselves.

The entire structure, save the administration building, is surrounded by a double concentric perimeter of two 16-foot chain-link fences sixty feet apart, topped by concertina wire. Access and egress for the complex are through a guarded, time-locked front entrance within the administration building and a rear sally port to receive new occupants when they are delivered.

The white cube building nearest the front entrance is devoted to support activities like cafeteria, gymnasium, library, and medical-dental clinics. The other three structures, known as the red, blue, and green buildings by their interior paint color, provide residential housing as well as classrooms and therapy locations. Each of the three is divided into a quadrant of four pods. These are high-ceilinged, pleasant common areas with skylights and floor-anchored tables in the center and what are called living quarters (not cells) lining the walls. Situated on the 87 square feet of each living space are a toilet, dresser, and bed. Its occupant can introduce added small floor pieces upon approval. The room's door can be locked from the inside but not the outside, except to protect personal belongings and when an emergency requires. A window in the door permits staff to conduct regular safety checks of residents.

No uniforms are worn. The incarcerated men are in civilian dress of their choosing, usually a jeans and t-shirt combination. The same is true with staff members, known as safety, security, or training technicians (not guards). Residents are free to access the recreation yard during scheduled times and the corridors when going to and from classes, therapy sessions, or appointments. An exception is the Red Zone, which is open to staff only.

A hierarchical system of earned privilege levels operates, with each person's status indicated by a mandatory color-coded name card. An *A* green card is the most favorable and allows unrestricted access to the library, art classes, recreation facilities and, commissary. *B* blue and *C* yellow cards allow successively reduced levels of access. Wearers of the lowest-status *D* red card—a small minority—are subject to extensive supervision but never solitary confinement. Privileges are earned based on progress in treatment and in institutional behavior.

No firearms or other weapons are allowed in the facility, even on the part of staff, including security personnel. When violence seems likely or erupts, it is responded to by verbal deescalation tactics. If these do not work, precise holding maneuvers are performed, followed by cool-off time periods and appropriate treatment team intervention. Each such event is fully documented and reported.

The census at this writing is 370 men. Female offenders are not currently in custody here but will be added in separated space when the expansion opens. To the dismay of Ms. Pechura and other Center leadership, some double upper-lower bunking has been introduced to provide additional beds for overflow. When it occurs, special care is taken not to pair highly aggressive men with more vulnerable individuals. Planning for the expansion includes making living quarters big enough to handle both beds on floor level.

In light of the absence of a set release date from civil commitment, the law requires that all residents for each of their first five years and every second year thereafter be given a formal hearing on whether commitment is still necessary. This is done before a judge with defense counsel, family members, and testifying experts present. Over time, approximately 170 residents have been released after scrupulous review. As the rate of incoming occupants is greater than the number outgoing, the population has continued to age over time, which has caused medical costs to soar. In the future, after the expansion of the facility, persons slated for conditional discharge will live in an adjacent Transition quarters now being planned to teach community living skills in order to enhance their likelihood of success.

Just as VCBR's custody practices are less authoritarian than the residents experienced in the penitentiary, its rehabilitation program is more rigid than found in the average therapy clinic. Although residents have the right not to participate in therapy programs, initial entry into VCBR is of course mandatory yet subject to numerous guidelines. Each month, the Department of Corrections determines which offenders currently in custody for code-designated qualifying violent sexual offenses are within 10 months of reaching the end of their sentence. The list is given to a commitment review committee composed of corrections officials, behavioral health department personnel (including at least one psychiatrist or psychologist), and the assistant or deputy attorney general of the Commonwealth. Names on the list are checked against a database of prison records and Static-99R psychological test scores to assess their relative risk to society.

The highest-risk cases are reviewed for placement options. Committee members vote on each case, and a recommendation for or against potential commitment is forwarded to the attorney general. This officer then decides whether to file a petition for civil commitment to circuit court. If so, the circuit judge holds a probable cause hearing on whether the defendant falls under the scope of the sexual predator code. A positive conclusion is followed by a formal trial, and the verdict of the judge or jury determines whether the offender in question is or is not committed to VCBR for treatment.[3]

The opposing bookend to mandatory commitment is that, once in VCBR, the resident cannot know when it will end—there is no set release date to look forward to. The stated mission of the institution is to rehabilitate all persons to which it is assigned so they can eventually be returned to society. Yet every individual in the program is unique; strenuous efforts are continuously made to have that happen, but release is never inevitable. Members of the staff conscientiously attempt to probe their charges' deepest feelings. Attitudes of denial or patterns of scheming against victims are noted. Group therapy is helpful here because, in their open discussions, group members will call out a member who does not admit committing a crime. Therapists press patients to accept the wrongness of attitudes that rationalized their unacceptable conduct. Did they seize opportunities offered for assault when they arose? Did they pretend to be "teaching" children about sex while hurting them for a lifetime?

Achieving such life-changing transformation in the human brain can require jolting actions. Polygraph tests are used to find out when patients lie.

Penile-plethysmograph assessments reveal arousal patterns. Staff observation of resident behavior enters the daily record of conduct. The VCBR career of each resident is tracked in terms of three levels of accomplishment: phase one—willingness to take charge of one's own recovery; phase two—owning up to troublesome thoughts and behaviors; and phase three—realizing what is required to risk moving on to a healthy life within the community.

In sum, in pursuing both its custodial role and treatment goal, VCBR seeks to contribute to human betterment. Individual freedom is sacrificed while self-knowledge is deepened. Self-absorption is replaced by becoming capable of giving relationships. Her *gentlemen*, as Ms. Pechura calls them, are not unredeemable monsters but assumed as salvageable.

The job is her calling. Stephanie defiantly rejects any professional stigma attached to serving sex offenders. When some charge VCBR is not tough enough on ex-convicts, she points to its record of no escapees from the facility.[4] When others attack it for not releasing enough residents, she talks of the valiant attempts to rewire flawed minds.

Ms. Pechura loves serving in her present position and is remarkably well suited for it in both advance preparation and personal traits. Perhaps most important of all, on a basic human level, this common bureaucrat regards her residents with tough-love respect and her colleagues with work-family affection. Even though only in mid-career, Stephanie has no desire to leave this special institution that performs such enormously difficult and important service in the fields of rural Virginia.

NOTES

1. Found in its current version at Virginia Code Title 37.2, Chapter 9, "Civil Commitment of Sexually Violent Predators."

2. Martin Andrews, "Boxed In: A Boy's Lost Week," *The Hook*, Issue 0204, January 30, 2003. Print reference retrieved online July 27, 2016.

3. Virginia Code § 9(37.2-900) through Virginia Code § 9(37.2-917).

4. One resident escaped while being transported to an outside medical appointment, however.

PART TWO

PUBLIC ENVIRONMENT

CINDY M. BERNDT, Regulation Expert

Unsung Heroine of Process

Photo by Charles T. Goodsell

We now turn in this study from the topic of public safety to that of public environment. Our first essay on this big subject is the battle for clean water, clean air, and safe waste disposal. It concerns regulation at the state level, which nowadays is the first line of defense. In this case, the common bureaucrat doing battle is in Virginia.

Regulation by the government of the private sector is not, as some believe, an unconstitutional seizure of power. It is carried out by means of a process grounded in law and reason. When Congress and state legislatures find themselves incapable of writing in the detail necessary to implement statutes, they authorize administrative agencies to issue regulations for this purpose. These rules are promulgated under guidelines set by statute and possess the force of law.

This process has been commonplace for decades and allows modern government to function—and in a form compatible with constitutional democracy. The formulation of regulations protects, for example, due process rights of notice and hearing. In Virginia, this is accomplished by the following steps: (1) posting of intent on the official website *Virginia Regulatory Town Hall*; (2) a waiting period for the governor and other executive officials to review that action; (3) a 30-day public comment period; (4) a 180-day period for changes made in response; (5) approval of a proposal by the administering organization; (6) a 60-day wait for public comments on this version; (7) a follow-up 180-day period for final language adjustments; (8) approval of the final version by that organization; and (9) an end-point delay of 30 days before going into effect.[1]

Environmental awareness in Virginia can be dated to 1906, when a bill was introduced in the General Assembly to require factories along its rivers to purify their discharges. It was not passed, leaving intact a situation one legislator described as the "God-given sewers of the State."

An initial first step in addressing this problem occurred in 1929, when the Virginia Department of Public Health began collecting water samples from 80 gauge stations along six state rivers. They were sent for analysis to Virginia Polytechnic Institute and Virginia Military Institute, resulting in the posting of signs alongside shoreline roads saying "water not potable." This worried municipal water officials because many towns drew their drinking water from the waterways. Stream pollution committees were formed to push for clean-up efforts and for construction of treatment plants.[2]

Little else was done on this front until 1946, when legislators meeting in Richmond decided to do something because of filth flowing through their capital city in the James River. On July 1 of that year, the General Assembly created the Virginia Water Control Board (VWCB) to address the problem on a statewide basis. This date may be considered the founding moment of modern environmental protection in the Commonwealth. It preceded by two years passage of the Federal Water Pollution Control Act—later known as the Clean Water Act.

The VWCB, which still exists as a key player in state matters, is a multi-member regulatory commission, not a hierarchical bureaucracy like the federal Environmental Protection Agency. It is made up of seven lay citizen members appointed by the governor for four-year staggered terms. VWCB members cannot be employed by the state and are unpaid except for expenses. However, they must possess some kind of background or knowledge about water matters. The statute advises that they come from occupations that include conservation, public health, business, and agriculture. Members do not represent a political party, and cannot have profited directly or indirectly from a board action for the past two years.

Initially, the VWCB operated with a small staff working out of an innocuous office building on Broad Street in west Richmond. Its purpose was to investigate and monitor water discharges from municipal treatment plants and industrial facilities, albeit without possessing enforcement power. However, by 1970, the environmental movement was emerging full swing across the country, stimulating the General Assembly to grant the VWCB enforcement authority. It also was allowed to double its staff so as to establish field offices around the state. Meanwhile, a new state constitution was adopted whose Article 11 declares it the policy of the state to "protect its atmosphere, lands, and waters from pollution, impairment or destruction for the benefit, enjoyment and general welfare of the people of the Commonwealth."[3]

This is the scene that existed at the VWCB in 1970. The newly created Enforcement Division needed an added secretary to work at its Richmond headquarters. One Cindy M. Berndt, a native of Richmond who held a newly acquired Associate of Arts degree in secretarial skills from Virginia Intermont College in Bristol, Virginia, saw the open position announcement. Like every college graduate, she needed a job. A search had yielded two offers. One was at the Medical College of Virginia (MCV) and the other at the Virginia Water Control Board. In deciding which one she would take, her reasoning was simple. The commuting distance to MCV was long and parking there was impossible, but VWCB offices were much closer to home and in a location where parking was ample. Hence, this young practical woman entered government not out of high principle but completely utilitarian needs. Little did she know, the choice would eventually end up taking her to a feeling of calling as a public servant.

For her first two years, Cindy performed ordinary secretarial duties for the Enforcement Division. But in typing reports and taking dictation, she began to pick up information on the steps and requirements of the enforcement process. She not only absorbed this new knowledge but asked what more she could do. This willingness to take the initiative was noticed by supervisors as an unusual attitude for a fresh-from-school secretary.

In 1972, Cindy was advanced to the position of Technician A, and she was asked to organize board meetings. The work involved preparing agendas, attending sessions, and writing up minutes and reports. Soon, she advanced to what amounted to a one-person secretariat to the board; after a time, she was the sole individual who knew all the technicalities of meetings and their documentation. This personal staff role was to continue and amplify in the coming decades, as we shall see.

In 1974, aspects of management began to supplement Cindy's board staff duties. Promoted to Technician B, she took on supervision of VWCB's professional service contracts. In five years, another promotion to Research Administrative

Officer A had her managing grants and contracts, with budget development and its accounting interface eventually thrown in. In 1980, just ten years after joining the Virginia Water Control Board, and with no formal training in public administration behind her, Cindy became its director of management services. Meanwhile, attending to daily board business remained in her hands.

Then, in 1984, Ms. Berndt was set in a direction toward what became her present-day responsibilities. She moved to the VWCB Policy Division and was given the title of agency regulatory coordinator. This move in effect placed her in the position of being *the* person to go to for information and advice on all the regulatory steps mentioned at the beginning of this essay. In addition, she watched over the administrative tools used to implement regulations, such as enforcement orders, the permitting of operations, the periodic reissuance of permits, preparation of service contracts, and the filing of applications for facility construction grants and loans. Still, the VWCB day-by-day staffing role continued. It is still with her today as the second piece of a career-long dual-job assignment.

Meanwhile, the environmental regulation picture in Virginia—as in the country as a whole—was expanding to include protection of other environmental media than water. In 1963, Congress passed the Clean Air Act, setting the nation firmly on the course of combating air pollution. Virginia responded in 1966 by enactment of an Air Pollution Control law that created an Air Pollution Control Board, modeled almost precisely after the Water Control Board. Congress began to address land pollution by means of the Solid Waste Management Act of 1965, and Virginia took on this mission in 1986 with the creation of a separate board for this purpose. This was the Waste Management Board, somewhat modeled after the Water Control Board. An attempt to coordinate these three separate regulatory bodies was attempted by forming a Council on the Environment. The Council was comprised of both citizen board chairs and civil service department heads working for the boards. The Council also reflected Virginia's citizen-oriented approach by including three private individuals as members.

The essence of this citizen-delegated, pluralized system of board administration lasted until the early 1990s. In 1991, the secretary of natural resources, Elizabeth H. Haskell, accepted the urging of environmental advocates and proposed uniting all four environmental entities into a unified whole. The expressed reason was not efficiency or economy, but a need to break down walls between domains whose actions are closely interconnected.

The process of unification was not easy. Conservationists and industry groups differed over many things having to do with the allocation of power. At the same time, each board sought to protect its own turf. Faced with this acrimony, an extensive joint planning project was mounted to pave the way toward resolution of differences. State officials and employees working in each medium joined representatives of all affected external parties to search for the best way to meld unity and link diversity. To tap the local government and community perspective, a Citizen's Advisory Group held six public meetings around the state. The sensitive matter of locating field offices was resolved by consolidating twenty-two field units into six regions.

Most importantly, serious attention was given not only to drafting an organization chart but actually changing attitudes in a holistic direction. By 1993, terms for the new administrative order were agreed upon and what is called the Virginia Department of Environmental Quality (DEQ) came into existence. It remains today as the prime mover in the state's environmental policymaking.[4]

Significantly, despite housing all environmental activity under one organizational roof, the three citizen boards remained intact, but embedded in the department as a whole. The statutory powers of each of the three were retained. They still set protection standards and enact or amend regulations according to state notice and hearing requirements. For this purpose, board members meet regularly in the General Assembly Building across from the Capitol, not at DEQ headquarters at 1111 East Main. In short, Virginia's unusual system of pluralized, citizen-body policymaking has in large part stayed in place. What the creation of DEQ did is to unify delegated enforcement activities, administer joint regulatory support systems, and take on cross-media functions such as Coastal Zone Management and joining other states to clean up the Chesapeake Bay.

Cindy has been a key actor in producing coherence within this organizational mix. Her pre-DEQ position of agency regulatory coordinator was converted to director of regulatory affairs. Directing rather than coordinating essentially the same thing as before has allowed realization of one of the reorganization's stated aims, achievement of "coordinated permit review and assistance."[5] In addition, public participation in the regulatory process was enhanced.

Looking at her career over time, Cindy Berndt has been central in carrying out Virginia's environmental laws for 48 years. This length of time constitutes two-thirds of the time such laws have existed (i.e., since 1946). Her service covers almost as much time before DEQ was established as it does after—23 years versus 25 at this writing. She has served under no less than four Water Control Board directors and seven Department of Environmental Quality directors. No one else in the present organization can match this record. Such longevity confers on her a singular status that is fully recognized in the organization and why she was recommended to be included in this book. Yet Cindy is a modest person who shuns notoriety, does tons of work from a small office without a secretary, and has become an agency legend as she approaches retirement. Let me try in short compass to summarize why.

Ms. Berndt did not begin her career as a conscious choice to join public service or work on environmental problems. Yet, from the very first day, she worked hard, asked for more duties regularly, and showed almost limitless capacity combined with utter dependability. Although formally educated in secretarial skills, her early supervisors discovered she would absorb the complexities of each assignment and retain them in her mind for future use. Her accumulated knowledge became an institutional asset, even more so as the amount of environmental regulation grew exponentially over the next decades.

She is opinionated but in a good way. Never hesitant to speak her mind, Cindy is famous for her blunt "No, you can't do that" assertions when a DEQ member asks about deviating from the rules or standard operating procedures. But since she explains her declarations clearly and points to exactly where the requirement comes from, no one can feel personally insulted. A convivial personality and quick easy laugh make bitterness impossible. Across the organization, she is known with affection as *the oracle*—an in-house Greek priestess purveying the will of the gods.

This trait of gatekeeper of procedural correctness does not mean Cindy is opposed to change. The very opposite is true; she relishes absorbing and implementing the ongoing flow of new environmental statutes and most recent federal mandates. Denying that she has any interest in making high policy, partisan policy shifts that occur at the governor's office or in the General Assembly are accepted philosophically as long as they are implemented correctly.

Environmental policymaking is, by its nature, controversial in America's capitalist society. Both advocates and opponents tend to be defiant. Within DEQ, the attitude is of course as a proponent of adequate environmental protection and the agency is proud of the record it has achieved in Virginia.[6] So it is not surprising that program people in headquarters and the regions can become excited about adding more potent standards to a given regulation or permit. This can set in motion a tendency to move too fast or cut corners here and there. When that happens, Cindy tells them she has absolutely no stake in the outcome of program goals, but knows that if the procedures followed to reach them are faulty in any way or not supported by law and regulation, the effort will be tied up in court for years. In short, she keeps a steady hand on the tiller even in turbulent waters.

Ms. Berndt serves the department well in another way. This is to act as a bridge across its separate elements. With her long familiarity with the procedures of each board, she can urge everyone to tolerate the working peculiarities of each. Flowing water is a controllable commodity that can be subject to downstream intervention and tangible improvement. Air emissions are escaped gasses that can be countered only at the source but never completely. Solid waste unavoidably expands with population growth and the only feasible objective is to maximize recycling and build sound landfills.

She also helps to bridge the gap between citizen board members meeting in the General Assembly Building and bureaucrats working at headquarters and in the regions. Her long experience with the boards allows her to remind agency people that these board members do not have the time and expertise possessed by full-time professionals, yet they have real power and must be respected. As for the interface in the opposite direction, she by her own acknowledgment knows "a little about lots of things" in regard to environmental protection generally in Virginia over the years, such as budgeting and accounting processes, service contracts and grants, and the management craft itself. This places her in a position whereby she can explain to citizen board members that there is a reason why the wheels of bureaucracy sometimes seem to turn slowly.

A final point is that one of Ms. Berndt's goals in upholding the rules has always been to insist that the ordinary citizens out there, the *Mary Janes* she calls them, have just as much opportunity to voice concern over pending permits or regulations as do big industrial or municipal interests. This consciousness for equity propelled her insistence that when board members held public meetings in Richmond or out in the state that they observe fairness in allocating comment time. Cindy has also supported steps taken within DEQ as a whole to compile and utilize an inventory of ways to increase citizen participation in agency decision making. After all, Article 11 states that protected air, lands, and waters are for the *people* of the Commonwealth.

In 2011, Cindy M. Berndt received the coveted Erchul Environmental Leadership Award at a ceremony on the campus of Virginia Military Institute in Lexington. It was conferred by vote of the membership of the Environment Virginia Symposium. This organization consists of hundreds of environmental experts from government and the private sector throughout the state. The award is named after a former professor of environmental science at VMI and has honored the movement's very top leaders. They picked Cindy from a pool of thirty nominees and the following tribute states why.[7]

> It is hard to imagine how environmental regulation could be effectively developed in Virginia without the expertise and leadership of Cindy Berndt. For 40 years, she has worked tirelessly at DEQ to help ensure that air, water, waste, and now renewable energy regulations are accurate, consistent, and legally sufficient. At any time of day (and often night as well), Cindy can be found advising and collaborating with her fellow DEQ staff members; members of the Air, Water, and Waste Boards; citizens from all different stakeholder groups, and even colleagues in other agencies and states. Her knowledge is encyclopedic; her generosity in sharing her expertise, limitless; her integrity and fairness, unquestionable; and her kindness and sense of humor, unequaled. Cindy has often been an *unsung hero* working expertly in the background. This award would help recognize her vital and inestimable contributions to environmental protection in our state.

NOTES

1. Virginia Department of Planning and Budget, Economic and Regulatory Analysis Division, "Standard Regulatory Process: Guide for State Agencies" (Richmond: Author, October 2014).

2. Virginia Department of Environmental Quality, *An Environmental History: Stories of Stewardship in Virginia* (Richmond: Author, 2008), 5–6.

3. Full Article text found in *An Environmental History*, 56. Virginia was one of the first states in the Union to do this.

4. *An Environmental History*, 14.

5. Virginia Department of Environmental Quality, "Environmental Management for the Twenty-First Century" (Richmond: Author, n.d.), 9.

6. See Virginia Department of Environmental Quality, *Celebrating 20 years: Stewardship, Sustainability, Solutions* (Richmond: Author, 2013), 9.

7. Text of Erchul Award tribute obtained from its recipient in e-mail dated February 2, 2017.

KAREN L. WILSON, Energy Advisor
The Public Policy Professional

This next common bureaucrat in our public environment section contrasts with the previous one. She occupies a staff position rather than line assignment, is concerned with policy content rather than process, and works on problems of energy rather than pollution. These differences give us pause to realize how complex this field of governance is.

Ms. Karen L. Wilson's formal job title is environmental scientist consultant senior, a phrase that could hardly be more misleading. She does not own a scientist's lab coat or work on a consultant's contract. For the moment, referring to her as main advisor to the director of Kentucky's Department for Energy Development and Independence will do, but even this broad characterization fails to capture the totality of her role.

Karen L. Wilson is a native daughter of the Bluegrass State, having been born in Louisville. Her father was an arborist in private practice and her mother a school-teacher. When Karen was six, her father bought a farm in Shelby County, a few miles to the east, and she still carries fond memories of doing barnyard chores. When it came time to attend college, she enrolled at the University of Kentucky in Lexington, fifty miles further east. She majored in English with a political science minor, although without showing any interest in public administration. Being good at writing allowed her to obtain part-time employment as an editorial assistant on campus.

After graduating in 1986, Ms. Wilson considered a graduate program in library science. However, a friend convinced her that her liberal arts background and writing ability would better be invested in a Master of Public Administration (MPA) program. She enrolled in one at the Martin School of Public Policy and Administration at the University of Kentucky at Lexington. In a course there on organization theory, the instructor illustrated points taken from health administration, and for a time she considered heading in that direction.

However, all plans changed when Karen was—unbeknownst to her—recommended by the Martin School faculty for an internship in Kentucky state government. The locale for this temporary employment was the Office of the Secretary for what was at the time the Natural Resources and Environmental Protection Cabinet (now the Energy and Environment Cabinet). This placed her at the state capital of Frankfort, some twenty miles back west.

The term "cabinet" in this context refers to a collection of related agencies within the larger array of state administrative organizations. Each is headed by a cabinet secretary. In this intern position, Karen found herself occupying a central role in the implementation of a new cabinet-wide customer service program. She surveyed agency personnel all across Frankfort, learned the details of related activities elsewhere in state government, and personally conducted employee training sessions. In retrospect, this assignment helped her to become acquainted with all corners of this governmental area, whose employees occupied no less than fifteen separate buildings around the state capital.

With this direct experience and an MPA concentration in environmental policy in hand, the way was well paved into regular employment in Kentucky state government. It has involved a myriad of activities, all the way from speech writing and media relations to policy research, project management, legislative liaison, and advisement of policymakers. Although Karen calls herself a generalist, this cliché belies the rich lode of substantive knowledge on energy and environmental matters that she has accumulated along the way.

During this time, she has remained in essentially one cabinet, although its name has changed more than once. Starting from when she was first hired, it has been called (1) Natural Resources and Environmental Protection (1996 to 2003 under Governor Paul Patton, Democrat); (2) Environmental and Public Protection (2003 to 2008 under Governor Ernie Fletcher, Republican); and (3) Energy and Environment (from 2008 onward under Governors Steve Beshear, Democrat, and Matt Bevin, Republican).

Karen's first port of call in this system was the Kentucky Division of Energy located within Natural Resources and Environmental Protection, where she remained for six years. The Division immediately took advantage of her communication skills. She was named public information officer and placed in charge of issuing press releases and organizing staff media interviews. Articles for the Cabinet's quarterly newsletter were written, and energy news items from all states were compiled and sent to *Conservation Update*, a magazine published by the National Renewable Energy Laboratory in Golden, Colorado.

Division programs in environmental education then became a priority. She sent speakers to schools and elsewhere to talk about the state's contribution to energy availability at low rates from carbon and renewable sources. She called upon corporate leaders of the construction, manufacturing, and retail sectors to promote the cause of energy efficiency. She took on the task of helping to introduce Kentucky to the Energy Star program, initiated in 1992 by the U.S. Department of Energy and Environmental Protection Agency. Its intent is to utilize the Star's logo mark to induce consumers to buy electrical appliances and other goods designed as meeting federal standards of energy efficiency. It is estimated that, nationwide, the program has achieved a 20 to 30 percent power savings in the products so identified.[1]

After six years on the job, Ms. Wilson's reputation as a fast learner and able manager had spread across the organization. This prompted, in 2003, a major shift in the direction of her career. She was elevated from division-level program operations to a series of executive support positions at high levels in Kentucky government. She occupied four of these in succession: (1) executive staff adviser to the commissioner of the Department of Environmental Protection within the Natural Resources and Environmental Protection Cabinet (during all of 2003); (2) staff adviser and assistant legislative liaison in the Office of the Secretary of that Cabinet (2004 to 2006); (3) assistant to the executive director within the Governor's Office of Energy Policy (2006 to 2008); and (4) chief of staff to the secretary of what had now become the Energy and Environment Cabinet (2008 to 2016). These assignments coincided with the administrations of Governors Fletcher and Beshear.

In essence, Karen Wilson had by now arrived at the top echelons of Kentucky's career civil service. After a first role as program manager and a second as facilitator for administrators, she was now in a position to benefit fully from her unusually broad experience across the organization.

Following the election of Republican Matt Bevin as governor in 2015, Ms. Wilson assumed her present assignment as policy adviser within the Department for Energy Development and Independence for the Energy and Environment Cabinet. This is a small unit that acts primarily as a think tank, research arm, and data collector for the Cabinet. Alongside this staff group in the Cabinet are two huge line departments of several hundred employees each, one for Environmental Protection and the other for Natural Resources. Now primarily a policy thinker, she is positioned at the center of a large bureaucracy responsible for big matters and connected to the top through her department head, Rick Bender, and from there, linked upward to Secretary Charles Snavely.

Although I do not wish to appear as though I am reducing our subject's work to a series of bullet points, I would like at this point in our essay to identify several standout characteristics of how Karen is fulfilling her current policy-thinking and planning role. Hence, the narrative switches from a chronological mode to an analytical one.

The first characteristic that comes to mind is that Karen is not an analyst in the narrow sense of evaluating policy performance or modeling the effect of policy changes. While familiar with all the optimizing analytic techniques based in economics and statistics, her head is not into number crunching. Instead, she is at the broad-gauge, big-picture level, driven by the normative goal of attaining adequate, dependable, and sustainable energy, including electric power generation for the citizens and industries of her state. "Energy is my passion," she once said in our conversations.

A second characteristic is that she has not gone from organization to organization selling her wares as an energy guru. She has remained loyal to her cabinet and its leaders over many years and anticipates remaining with it for the rest of her career. When asked where that may lead, she mentioned attaining more depth of knowledge in the substantive issues and technical aspects of the many moving parts of this complex field.

Third, her normative bent and organizational stability have led to a personal commitment to a vision for where Kentucky's energy policy posture should move. It is not a viewpoint that she alone harbors, but rather, the outcome of discussions throughout the organization over time. Its centerpiece is the notion that the Commonwealth must lead from its coal-producing strength and not be caught in the economic trap of depending solely on cheap natural gas or relying only on the currently small output of the renewable sector. The answer in her thinking is to collaborate and work with colleagues in developing a comprehensive, balanced, and constantly shifting strategy that continuously adopts to prevailing market and political forces. This must be accompanied by taking advantage of all technologies that become available to conserve available fuels, generate cheaper long-term alternative sources, and take advantage of future energy storage opportunities. More near-term steps within the department include integrating energy conservation with both energy production and consumption; helping to educate the public, business, and local governments about energy efficiency and alternative energy opportunities; maintaining ongoing databases on energy sources, production, employment, and consumption; tracking the costs, reliability, and sustainability of fossil and renewable power generation; and working as a team member to keep informed of the latest technological developments in the field.

A fourth feature of Ms. Wilson's policy work has been that she has been able to act on this vision. This opportunity arose when she was asked to take charge of preparing an application for Kentucky's admission to join what is known as the Policy Academy on Power Sector Modernization, sponsored by the National Governors Association (NGA) located in Washington, D.C. Karen was chosen as point person for the whole undertaking, including preparation of documents to support the application. Eventually, Kentucky was accepted into the Academy, where it joined Rhode Island, Washington, and Oregon.

What the Academy consists of is a series of organized conversations over time and among energy officials of the four states, facilitated by NGA staff. Each state participates individually in seeking solutions to its own identified series of policy challenges and directions. For its part, Kentucky wishes to engage with a broad section of stakeholders in the process of learning about what each state is doing in the energy area and discuss new possibilities over the horizon. To that last point, Karen, in her application, stressed the need to develop new ideas. In the governor's cover letter to the National Governors Association, which she drafted, the following passage is found:

> We learned from the shale boom that the nation's energy trajectory is unpredictable. The important lesson is that flexible policies based on what is possible, not what is pre-determined, can help create unimagined opportunities. So while we might not be able to predict the next big thing that will upend the energy landscape, and while we cannot shape any number of external forces that have an impact on our economy and use of our energy resources, we can and must be forward-looking, prudent in our decision-making, and open to ideas and a broad array of viewpoints, perspectives, and areas of expertise.[2]

A fifth central theme is a readiness to consult colleagues. In a matter as complex as state energy policy, no single individual can possibly be informed on all aspects. While over the decades Karen has acquired an informed overview, she knows enough to know what she does not know. When launching a study of any important subject, she invariably assembles a team. This brings more complete facts to the table, but even better than that, it brings contrasting perspectives. To formulate the Policy Academy application, she identified a team of seventeen persons including administrators and staff from throughout the Energy and Environment Cabinet, personnel from the Economic Development Cabinet, administrators of the Kentucky Emergency Management Agency, and key officials from the Governor's Office.[3]

A factor that has been helpful to teamwork is a physical move of the Cabinet in 2016, from numerous buildings throughout town to a single structure on the outskirts of Frankfort, set in a large new office park. Called *The 300* for its address on the park's entry road, Sower Boulevard, the edifice consists of a roughly 500 × 250-foot white block structure five stories high. It is LEED certified (i.e., Leadership in Energy and Environmental Design), and as such, it boasts a white noise instillation inside and a mile-long exercise track outside.

Primary circulation space consists of a set of two 10-foot-wide corridors running the full length of the building on all five floors, each intersected by a trio of generous common areas. This arrangement has made personal interaction and collaboration easy among the thousand-plus daily occupants. Indeed, select groups are in the habit of meeting regularly in their nearby commons, and staff use the spectacular corridors as a venue for in-motion meetings at a walking gait.

Sixth, Karen is careful to keep important affected stakeholders informed on pending plans. This of course has it dangers, such as making it possible for powerful external actors to gain privileged insights or exercise undue influence. At the other end of the influence spectrum, the involvement of casual observers energized by social media could bog down proceedings and waste everyone's time.

What Karen and colleagues attempt is to achieve a midway course between capture and overload. They seek to maintain continuing close ties with representatives of organizations that are vitally affected and whose cooperation is essential for success. Those invited constitute a range of groups with varied constituencies and hence viewpoint tendencies. This spread promotes an even-handed set of different and even opposing policy preferences. For her Policy Academy application Karen invited investor-owned utilities, electricity-generating cooperatives, industrial utility customers, energy service providers, the Kentucky Municipal Utilities Association, the state Conservation Committee, the state Housing Corporation, and many other organizations.

A seventh and final characteristic of Ms. Wilson's work concerns the personal influence she has over policy outcomes. When discussing this matter with her, she made a big point of saying her personal extent of influence is not an issue; the point is to advance policy success, not to control its formulation. Her attitude seemed notable to me in that I have seen how many policy experts and for-hire consultants automatically assume they *know* what is best for the organization, otherwise they would not be paid such substantial fees. One could even carry this argument further and suggest the entire public policy industry is sold on the proposition that its practitioners tell the *truth* to power. As for Ms. Wilson, I detect in her an aura of poised humility that has gained, over time, widespread respect as she walks and talks the hallways of The 300.

It is my belief that those of us who have taught and done policy analysis could benefit significantly from absorbing into our own thinking the seven principles of Karen's work life. In fact, one could say they could spell out an attractive model by which to describe a good or even ideal public policy professional. I repeat them here:

The good policy professional

- realizes the heart of policy work is not number crunching but thinking long, hard, and deep about satisfying a vital public need;

- is not a roving consultant going from door to door but a loyal organization member who is around for a long time;

- comes to the organization's problems not with an attitude of technical neutrality but a shared normative vision to advance;

- is able to act in a tangible way to advance the vision, especially by generating fresh ideas;

- is anxious to consult with knowledgeable colleagues within the organization and stress teamwork;

- is always careful to hear, respect, and respond to concerns of heavily involved external stakeholders that hold alternative views; and

- realizes full well that the point of doing public policy work is not to get one's own conclusions adopted but to advance policy success.

NOTES

1. *Wikipedia, The Free Encyclopedia*, "Energy Star," retrieved online May 29, 2017, https://en.wikipedia.org/wiki/Energy_Star.

2. Governor Matthew G. Bevin to Aliza Wasserman, "National Governors Association," November 18, 2016.

3. Kentucky Department for Energy Development and Independence, "NGA Policy Academy on Power Sector Modernization: Application from the Commonwealth of Kentucky," November 18, 2016.

HOWARD W. GLENN, Drainage Master
Coaching a Team That Must Win

Photo by Charles T. Goodsell

This common bureaucrat receives fanfare for keeping Richmond dry. He is responsible for making sure its sewers do not overflow, heavy rain does not fill its streets, and the James River stays within its banks. This is the kind of crucial work government does that is almost completely unknown to the public—except when sewers back up, runoff stops traffic, or one's city floods.

It was an early April morning when Howard W. Glenn picked me up at my hotel. He was dressed in casual work clothes with a broad grin on his face. We got in his pickup and drove south on U.S. 1 across the James River into an industrial area. After many twists and turns, we entered a gigantic works yard full of motorized equipment, pieces of concrete conduit, and long street poles. Parking in front of a brick structure marked "Department of Public Utilities and Operations Building," a quick elevator ride took us to the second floor, where we entered a large open room filled with desks and abuzz with activity. I was in the operational headquarters of Richmond's drainage master.

Yet the room had no aura of imperious authority—only a bunch of men and women chatting amiably as they geared up for the day's work. They immediately took notice of the visiting stranger, and many came up to greet me. On a table in the middle of the crowded room, an old but inflated football was positioned upright on a stand. I asked Mr. Glenn if its purpose was for off-duty employee recreation. He replied sometimes, but mainly to be there as a tangible symbol of what I was encountering: a spirited *team* preparing to launch yet another day's contest with water—absolutely essential to any city and dangerous if the opponent gets out of hand.

He led me to his small office, distinguished by a fake street sign above the door stating *Stormwater Ave*. Soon we were on a first-name basis and talking about his life and career. He grew up in Richmond, the second of three brothers and two sisters. The family was big due to the unusual circumstance of parents that divorced, remarried, and then divorced a second time to remarry their original spouses. Nonetheless, everyone in Howard's extended family remains closely in touch and devoted to each other.

His biological father (Edwin Smith) was a fireman in populous Henrico County, a large urban area just east of the city. After years of serving on a force of more than 500, he advanced to the rank of fire chief, the first and only African American to do so. It was, Howard explained, his dad's outgoing personality and determination to serve others, coupled with his mother's independence and thirst for knowledge, that have inspired his own personal development.

After attending Bryant and Stratton Academy in Richmond, Howard sought and obtained a job in the city's Parks and Recreation Department. At first, he was employed as a seasonal recreation worker and groundskeeper. Later, he was assigned full-time to park maintenance generally. The young man's performance in this capacity led to his becoming supervisor of grass cutting throughout the city's large park system.

After two years, he joined Richmond's Department of Public Works, and for four years, he worked on the construction, drainage, and maintenance of residential streets and arterial roadways. While in this job, he enrolled in training courses that resulted in certifications in Asphalt Cement, Soils and Aggregate, and Pavement Marking. In 1998, the department widened his responsibilities to include water drainage, not only from road surfaces but across city terrain as a whole. For the next six years, Howard accumulated detailed field knowledge of how best to control surface water, an experience that in retrospect prepared him for his present position. His final assignment in Public Works was to manage all public works facilities south of the James River. Meanwhile he was taking courses at J. Sergeant Reynolds Community College to supplement his growing mastery of the city's infrastructure.

Mr. Glenn's next move upward came in 2009, when all drainage functions were transferred from Public Works to the city's Department of Public Utilities (DPU). Unlike Public Works, it is a self-financing public enterprise with 750 employees that care for hundreds of millions of dollars' worth of assets and collect over $300 million per year for doing so. DPU's enterprises include the nation's eighth largest natural gas utility, an electric power distribution network, a drinking water treatment and supply system, two water treatment plants, and a section responsible for street lighting.[1]

Howard's first job at DPU was superintendent of the stormwater maintenance program. Its task was to keep rain run-off conveyance channels clear. Around this time, large communities around the nation were realizing that something had to be done about stormwater and its drainage. The U.S. Environmental Protection Agency had entered the field and adopted regulations and grant programs. The heart of the problem is that as municipalities grow, more and more of their land area is covered with impermeable surfaces like streets and shopping centers. This means surface water does not filtrate into the ground quickly but flows wherever it can, regardless of what harm it does to property. Eventually, it reaches streams and can pollute them as well as causing soil erosion and the possibility of flash floods.

Stormwater floods had occurred in the past in Richmond. On September 1, 2004, torrential rains brought in by Tropical Storm Gaston hit the historic downtown as well as commercial areas across the metro area. Sinkholes opened up to swallow cars. Even where street surfaces were still intact, hundreds of people were trapped in their cars. Five were killed, and Governor Mark R. Warner declared an emergency.[2]

As stormwater maintenance superintendent, Howard was determined that Richmond would not suffer another Gaston disaster. He acquired a Storm Water Inspection Certificate and took on the task of organizing a suitable protection program. He and others in DPU drew up plans for ditch, gutter, and easement monitoring and related infrastructure construction projects.

DPU accepted the challenge organizationally by creating a new division, called the Stormwater Utility, to deal with the safe diversion of stormwater on a user fee basis. This called for land use regulation while Howard's jurisdiction was, at the time, collection and conveyance of the water to the stormwater treatment plant on the James River. Eventually, the two programs were merged. Then, since in older parts of Richmond both stormwater and sanitary sewage are removed by the same piping system, it was also logical for Howard to become responsible for collection and conveyance of all sanitary waste water to its treatment plant on the James.

As it turned out, this combined program activity became the core of Mr. Glenn's current organization with one exception. This is a third DPU water-related mission, management of a floodwall that had been built along both banks of the James River. In effect, the existence of the floodwall expands the task of Richmond water drainage severalfold in that a vast natural catchment area is created by a natural watershed extending deep into the Appalachian mountain chain.

Flood prevention, along with stormwater control and all channeled water collection, came together under Mr. Glenn's leadership in 2016 as the Stormwater, Waste Water, and Floodwall Division of DPU. Technically, he is acting deputy director for stormwater matters, operations manager of all piped water collection, and de facto chief of floodwall management. Within the Department of Public Utilities itself, he holds the rank of Acting Director II. But regardless of titles, the division is his baby and he has built it into one unified team which he coaches.

To clarify the importance of each of his unit's three drainage missions, I shall now outline in some detail what each one involves.

The waste water mission is the oldest of the three responsibilities. Some of the brick tunnels leading to the waste water treatment plant along the river are large enough to drive a truck through, and there is no doubt that they are over a century old. Richmond's waste water system as a whole is rated at a capacity of seventy MGD (million gallons per day), making it what the industry calls a Phase II type. Collection mains leading to the treatment plant range from six to 48 inches in diameter. In its entirety, the network is approximately 1,500 miles in length. This includes laterals, the lines that connect individual buildings to street mains.

Management of the waste water system is an ongoing task. Preventative maintenance is needed to avoid surprise sewage back-ups and overflow, a situation that endangers public health and infuriates citizens. Upward of 250 pipe breaks can occur annually, and each must be fixed immediately. Since the system is underground, it cannot be directly inspected, and indirect methods are needed, such as threading video cameras through the pipes or pumping fog into them to see from which manholes it exits. Sedimentation and solids must be removed from screens and filters. Sewage emanating from restaurants is a particular problem since their grease traps and oil-water separators are often poorly cleaned. Long-term work includes laying pipe in new subdivisions, updating manhole records with respect to depth and direction of flow, converting paper network construction maps to electronic form, and renewing permits granted previously by the Virginia Water Control Board.

The stormwater mission is a different ballgame. Its infrastructure is mainly above ground. Compared to waste water's 1,500 miles of pipe, it has only 200 miles— but that is made up for by 800 miles of street gutters, road ditches, and drainage channels. Also, Howard's personal relationship to the system is not the same; he had worked in the stormwater area for several years in Public Works. As noted, he entered the field after it had emerged as a major policy issue area and was a principal planner and builder of the present system. In this sense, it is his favorite grandchild, so to speak, and he runs it with gusto from his office on *Stormwater Ave.*, along with a staff of thirty-five men and women.

As with waste water, stormwater channels must be clear. Since they are usually on the ground's surface, preventative inspection every three years is done not by video or fog programs but by meticulous observation and probing. Between times, and regularly after every substantial storm, crews go out and remove trash from gutters, clear ditches of debris, and unclog inlets. With over 35,000 storm basins to collect overflow, a substantial number need cleaning every time. Only this way will the system's 50–70 MDG capacity be sustainable.

Although no longer called a utility, this relatively new program is still self-financed through user fees. Monthly amounts are indicated on DPU utility bills sent to its 60,000 customers. They can be substantial, especially for commercial and industrial enterprises. Hence, it is important that citizens feel they are getting something back for their money. Public confidence in the system has been sought in two ways.

One is to operate a public communication channel known as the Customer Complaint System for stormwater. A citizen with a problem accesses it by means of phone or computer. The information received regarding time, location, and nature of the problem is recorded electronically. The ten to as many as forty complaints received each day (many more if it is a wet one) are reviewed to ensure that responses proceed promptly in order of priority. The data are automatically entered into a general "CityWorks" digital platform to ensure that final follow-through is complete.

A second way is a four-year public education program sponsored by DPU but dealing mainly with stormwater. Called RVA H2O, it was sparked by an EPA program to encourage community outreach. Talks were given to civic clubs, schools, and churches. Green alley and stream restoration projects being undertaken were described. Community clean-ups were organized and "It's Your River" billboards posted in English and Spanish. Briefings were held on the use of rain barrels, rain gardens, grass swales, and wet ponds. The most colorful piece of the campaign was a competition among area artists to paint murals on street sewer inlets; Howard showed me one, and I could not resist photographing it.

The third major responsibility of our Drainage Master is to maintain and operate the James River Floodwall. Over time, Richmond's identity has been intimately tied to the James River. Even the city's name comes from the river; early English settlers christened it *Richmond* because the view of the James from its banks was strikingly similar to the view of the Thames River from Richmond Hill in England. Like the Thames in Britain, the Virginia waterway was crucial to early settlement and commerce and is celebrated as a resource for sport and enjoyment.

However, draining as it does a huge western watershed, the beloved James has repeatedly flooded America's Richmond Hill. The first known case occurred in 1771. The number since 1816, is no less than 178. While half of these were minor, several have been serious and a few catastrophic. The worst occurred in 1972 as a consequence of Hurricane Agnes, which brought 16 inches of rain in Virginia during a 36-hour period. Enormous damage was done, including a virtually complete wipeout of the stores, restaurants, and tobacco warehouses in Shockoe Slip and Shockoe Bottom, the city's main tourist and restaurant areas.[3]

Pressure to take drastic antiflood action did not emerge, however, until November 7, 1985. Heavy rains, generated by Hurricane Juan caused the river to crest at 24.77 feet. Damage was widespread and unusually severe, setting in motion a drive to build a floodwall. The Army Corps of Engineers was commissioned to do so, and by October 21, 1994, it was dedicated. A total of 3.2 miles of wall were constructed, approximately one mile on the North side and a bit over two miles on the South bank. The project, made of concrete, steel, stone, riprap, and earth, cost $140 million. It is designed to hold back a flood crest up to 31 feet and provide 280-year risk protection to 700 hundred acres of flood plain. A flood capable of testing these specifications has not occurred since.

Nonetheless, it is imperative to keep the structure well maintained. While several units of DPU contribute to this end, Howard's employees bear the brunt of the work. Since any loosening of wall elements over time could be fatal, Survey Reference Plates affixed to each of the wall's vertical monoliths are checked within a hundredth of a foot by special instruments for adherence to exact elevation and verticality standards. Since the wall embraces a park and is a popular tourist attraction, debris and litter must be picked up, graffiti removed, and grass mowed in the summer. The wall has numerous gates for use by trains, trucks, cars, pedestrians, and pipelines. For safety's sake, none of these are power operated. So if a flood is approaching, much manpower is needed to seal off the city. Once a summer on "Closing Day" all gates are maneuvered shut in a publicized ritual. Following this yearly exercise, the Corps of Engineers comes to review results and inspect the wall.

All this is fine, I told our Drainage Master. But how do you know when a flood is on the way? Easy, he replied: When the hydrologists stationed upstream at the river towns of Wingina and Cartersville say the water is rising at X rate, you just pull the trigger—and in 48 hours, you'll be ready for a hit.

I employ in the title to this essay the metaphor of needing to *win*. We now know what that refers to: the absolute necessity to protect a million people from the disasters of (1) raw sewage, (2) torrential rains, and (3) an out-of-control river.

Although Mr. Howard W. Glenn bears the responsibility of keeping Richmond dry, he does not take on this task alone. He relies on a *team* of seventy-five men and women. That word is the right one not just because of Howard's office football but what he does every day as the organization's coach.

One thing he does is to connect personally with each individual serving under him. During the day when we were driving around the city in his truck, at almost every corner we encountered a worker of his on duty. He or she and Howard would wave at each other and yell a greeting. Every time a person on the team has a birthday, Howard sends a birthday card that arrives on time. When an employee completes a project or passes a milestone, he or she receives public recognition with a signed certificate of appreciation. At retirement parties, a faux street sign is presented bearing the person's last name. Persons showing potential in a technical specialty are sent to the appropriate training course, similar to what he had when he was young. In support of the advance of female management opportunity, he sends promising young women workers to attend the Virginia Commonwealth University Leadership Institute, headed by his wife.

Another trick of Coach Glenn is to build morale in group settings. Twice a month, his players gather for an all-hands safety meeting. They begin promptly at 7:30 a.m. and last through lunch. Topics range from chainsaw safety to how not to contract the flu or West Nile virus. Summer picnics, boat trips, and bowling tournaments permit intra-team personal friendships to grow. Howard designed a logo for the division that has never been approved by higher-ups, but nonetheless is displayed everywhere. It features an abstraction of a blue stormwater umbrella, a green collections conduit, and a gray floodwall monolith, all encircled as three-in-one.

Howard's coaching takes on an authentic air because of the personal interest he takes in the precise details of the work he is supervising. One morning, he took me to see a water diversion facility the size of an indoor football field. He had hoped overnight rains would be collecting there to demonstrate its holding capacity, but it was empty. However, he used the occasion to assure the workers on duty that a sediment lift they had ordered is on the way. That afternoon, Howard received word that a Public Works worker supervising repaving of a street wanted to see him. We drove to Gordon Avenue in south Richmond, and while I waited, he took nearly an hour to show his colleague exactly how the extra layer of asphalt could be applied without restricting the flow of stormwater into curb inlets.

At another point in my visit, Howard could not resist taking me to a reconstruction building site on Commerce Road. The emerging new structure will accommodate all three missions of the division under one roof. In addition, it will provide space for an adjoining set of laboratories where both waste water and stormwater will be tested. Each lab will use different techniques to look for different contaminants, he explained, but it will be helpful for the two sets of technicians to interact directly and compare results.

Personally, Mr. Glenn is a calm, experienced, and highly knowledgeable public servant. He is a natural leader, an innovative thinker, and a total professional. To his credit, he has ascended in level of responsibility in Richmond City Government through dedicated hard work, not prior credentials or insider contacts. He has proudly carried on the legacy of an African American fire chief father who went to the top in the former capital of the Confederacy. When I asked Howard about the future, his quiet answer was that someday the word *acting* will disappear from his title and perhaps even the term *deputy*.

My advice to residents of Richmond: Watch this public servant. He is going places.

NOTES

1. Richmond Department of Public Utilities, *Annual Report 2015-2016*, retrieved online June 27, 2017.

2. Associated Press, "Five People Die, Many More Homeless and Powerless," retrieved online June 20, 2017.

3. Henrico County, "Historic Floods: James River near Richmond, Virginia," and Henrico County, "Top Ten Highest Historical Crests: James River near Richmond," both accessed June 27, 2016. On the 1771 incident, see Mary Tyler-McGraw, *At the Falls: Richmond, Virginia and Its People* (Chapel Hill: University of North Carolina Press, 1994), 54–56.

PART THREE

PUBLIC CONSERVATION

DANIEL W. MCKEAGUE, Forest Ranger

In the Habit of Change

Photo by Charles T. Goodsell

We now turn to the general topic of Public Conservation. Two of the great public administration stories on this subject to be told are the creation of the National Park Service and the United States Forest Service, both of which were a product of the Progressive Era. The first story is about conserving precious parklands and cultural sites for public education and enjoyment. The second one is about conserving vast public forest lands in order to protect wildlife, harvest timber, and offer opportunities for sport and spiritual renewal. I told the Park Service story once in a previous place; aspects of the Forest Service story are told below.[1]

Shortly after first sitting down to talk with our subject, Dan McKeague, he shared a casual observation about his organization that I now realize is more important than I thought at the time. He commented that at Forest Service retirement parties where multiple generations of employees mix, jokes are told about how the members of each successive generation talk differently about their experience. Newer employees are optimistic about the agency's prospects; midcareer people are hopeful but nonetheless cautious; and the older generation and retirees see the agency as going to the dogs.

What this variation reveals is a government bureau that is the very opposite of mired in a permanent status quo. Instead it is constantly changing. As understanding of the complexities of varied species, climates, soils, and terrains of forests deepens, knowledge of what precise interventions the agency should make in their natural systems grows. Beyond a developing science, however, lies a varied and changing array of political demands from the agency's constituents. Over the decades, the Forest Service has been severely criticized for practices relating to timbering, fire suppression, pest control, and wildlife, but to its credit has adopted major policy changes in all these areas. When this happens, agency veterans are aghast that their views of good work have been tossed aside. At the other end of the spectrum, newcomers are enthusiastic about seeing new ideas replace the old ones. People like Dan—who stand at neither pole but are sympathetic to the newcomers—are philosophical, telling academics who show up at their door that it's always this way—the agency has gotten into a permanent habit of change.

Mr. Daniel W. McKeague (pronounced "Mick Keg"), at 32, is probably the youngest of the Forest Service's 600-some district rangers. His background is unusual and varied. Born of a Cuban mother and a New Zealand father, Dan is proud of his cosmopolitan heritage. It appears to have pointed him in the direction of public service. As a college student at the University of Florida, the district ranger of the Ocala National Forest came one day to speak in one of his classes. Dan was inspired enough to decide then and there to pursue a career in this field.

Not simply content with taking courses on the subject, he sought short-term jobs to acquire experiential learning in varied roles. He worked as a backcountry ranger assistant in Alaska, special conservation projects manager in New Zealand, recreation program leader for the University of Florida, and geographic information system analyst for a local water management district.

Upon receiving a B.S. degree in forest resources and conservation in 2007, Dan embarked on an M.S. degree in planning at Florida State, specializing in environmental planning and natural resource management. During his graduate student years, he again sought collateral employment, this time as environmental planner for the Florida Trail Association. Following graduation in 2009, he continued work at this nonprofit organization as coordinator of land acquisition for the Florida National Scenic Trail.

In October 2011, Dan obtained a position in what he considered the ultimate possibility, the U.S. Forest Service. His first assignment was at the national forests headquarters for Florida, where as a GS-11 he served as acting program manager for forest lands and minerals. In this capacity he sat on a unified budget steering committee, supervised a boundary survey program, and created a Web-based GIS system for public and internal viewing. After 15 months here he was transferred to Florida's Apalachicola National Forest, where he became acting district staff officer for recreation, trails, and wilderness areas. His five months in the position exposed him to the management side of forestry. He hired and supervised team employees and developed plans for using Americorps volunteers to help maintain camp and trail facilities.

In October 2012, he shifted from temporary acting assignments to a regular posting at the Pacific Southwest Regional office of the Forest Service in Vallejo, California. At the rank of GS-13, he became a program manager for Cooperative Forestry, which is the name for the Forest Service's provision of stewardship assistance to the care of millions of acres of private and state-owned forest land around the country. In this capacity, he supervised with state and local partners three programs in California, Hawaii, and the Pacific Islands: Forest Legacy, Forest Stewardship, and Community Forests. The job involved extensive collaboration across governmental jurisdictions and between the agency and private partners.

Dan's record in these Forest Service positions over a period of just four years led to his appointment, in June 2015, to lead the Eastern Divide Ranger District. At the time, his new boss, Tom Speaks, the forest supervisor for the Jefferson and nearby George Washington National Forest, stated, "Dan brings a wealth of experience in land management and enjoys working with communities and that's why he is a great fit for the Eastern Divide Ranger District."[2]

The position of district ranger that Dan now occupies calls for clarification. It is the prime responsible field officer of the organization. The cadre of district rangers form the front lines of its direct operations across the country. The term *ranger* was adopted in the early history of the Forest Service as a counter to the *agent* of the 19th-century General Land Office (GLO). This was a highly politicized powerhouse in the Department of the Interior that surveyed and sold public lands as fast as possible to timber and mining companies and later distributed them free to homesteaders. Gifford Pinchot, an analyst in the GLO's Washington office, became alarmed that precious forest resources were being devastated by the actions of his employer. Later, when President Grover Cleveland set aside many western lands as protected reserves, Pinchot became a special *forest* agent to investigate how the forests on them could be conserved. A Division of Forestry was formed, and Pinchot became its head after Theodore Roosevelt assumed the presidency in 1901. Pinchot convinced Roosevelt to elevate the Division of Forestry to bureau status, and in 1905, it was transferred to the Department of Agriculture and renamed the Forest Service with Pinchot named chief forester.[3]

In this position, Pinchot's primary attention was focused on what was going on in the field and not just Washington. Accordingly, he formed a body of sturdy male forest rangers to occupy the lands themselves in order to keep Land Office agents and their corporate cronies from misusing the land. These individuals were hardy souls that, when furnished with a horse, tent, and gun, had the responsibility of fighting off land predators so as to impose some degree of protection.

This image of the lonely outdoor guardian of the public good has since passed into Forest Service culture as the mythic device by which to battle for Pinchot's utilitarian ideal of achieving "the greatest good for the greatest number over the longest time." Today, the forest ranger no longer rides alone with his horse but instead commands a modern administrative organization. Yet, still today, the man or woman occupying this position is endowed, personally, with continuously standing initial authority to make all decisions necessary—in the words of the agency motto—in behalf of "caring for the land and serving people."[4]

In 1960, public administration scholar Herbert Kaufman published a book titled *The Forest Ranger*. In it, he brilliantly describes how the institutional environment of the ranger was structured at that time. In organizing his Forest Service, Pinchot had two opposing objectives: to forge a unified approach to conserving this vital resource of the nation and yet grant wide local latitude to its ranger managers. His insistence on autonomy in the field sprang from his firm belief that employees in Washington could have no idea what was actually going on in the woods and hence should not be allowed to restrict or control operations. Individual Forest Service districts vary greatly and issues of administration are fast moving. Moreover, rangers were widely scattered often to isolated places, denying the organization the benefit of office propinquity to aid coordination.

Pinchot thus built a system of decentralization that was real yet controlled. Its control devices included methods used in all bureaucracies, such as advance submittal of plans, informal decision clearance, post hoc inspections, and a unifying culture. However, two novel devices were introduced. One was the requirement that rangers keep daily diaries of their actions. These journals could not be later altered and were periodically submitted for review. The other was a system of *pre-formed* decisions whereby numerous generic problem situations were written up and published in a manual. Each contained instructional guidelines on how to proceed when and if that type of problem arises. The opportunity for ranger discretion stemmed from making a choice as to which, if any, scenario applies. The result, Kaufman concludes, avoided a military-style hierarchy yet allowed significant field autonomy and a sense of local command.[5] While both of these administrative tools have since been discarded, an unusually high degree of self-containment on the part of individual forest districts still remains.

The Forest Service's creation in 1905 was accomplished not by a formal organic statute enacted by Congress but rather by a Transfer Act that shifted responsibility for western forest reserves from the Department of Interior to the Department of Agriculture. Oddly enough, even its name was not openly declared by Congress but acquired by use: when the initial pertinent agricultural appropriation act was drafted, the words *Bureau of Forestry* had somehow been replaced by *Forest Service.*[6]

Despite this low-key birth, the agency has, over a century-plus, grown to a $5 billion enterprise that employs 33,000 personnel. It manages 193 million acres of forest and grassland in forty-four states and territories, operates eighty experimental forests, and runs twenty-eight Job Corps Civilian Conservation Centers. More than half of the nation's fresh water flows from forest lands that the agency affects directly or indirectly.

The Forest Service is divided into three quite different parts. The most important is National Forests and Grasslands, which administers the country's 154 national forests and twenty grasslands. One of these units, the Jefferson National Forest, includes Dan's bailiwick. It is in Region Eight of what is known as the National Forest System. The System employs a third of the agency workforce, with roughly another third available for wildfire work when needed. Including capital spending and land acquisition, this piece of the institution consumes 77 percent of its budget.[7]

Forest and Rangeland Research is the agency's science arm. It comprises seven research units, including a Forest Products Laboratory and an International Institute for Tropical Forestry. Deliberately made independent of National Forests and Grasslands so that current agency thinking does not inhibit new research, it is staffed by 500 scientists and 1,400 support personnel. The third component, State and Private Forestry, cooperates with state and local governments, private forest owners, and forest product industries to promote good land stewardship. It was here that Dan McKeague was employed just prior to his appointment as district ranger.

The Jefferson National Forest comprises 726,757 acres, located in nineteen counties of southwestern Virginia, with small projections into West Virginia and Kentucky. It was established in 1936, in accord with the Weeks Act of 1911, which allowed purchase of lands within the watersheds of navigable rivers on the pretense it would lay the basis for power dams. In effect, however, it became a vehicle for extending the Forest Service's jurisdiction to the eastern United States. The statute enabled the Jefferson Forest and its companion, the George Washington National Forest, to be established on eroded former timber land in the hopes of generating jobs and income in Depression-afflicted rural Virginia.

Dan, as district ranger, is responsible for approximately 400,000 acres in the Jefferson Forest, an area designated as the Eastern Divide District. Its name comes from the fact that it sits astride watersheds emptying to the east and west (i.e., the Atlantic Ocean and Gulf of Mexico, respectively). Eastern Divide is one of eight districts in the administratively combined George Washington and Jefferson National

Forests. Its terrain consists of lengthy stretches of ridge and valley along the Appalachian chain stretching from Wythville, Virginia, to near Covington, including parts of eleven Virginia counties as well as Monroe County in West Virginia. Several areas designated as *wilderness* are contained within it, protected by law for posterity. The district is transected by some 700 miles of Forest Service road and 150 miles of the Appalachian Trail. Eastern Divide headquarters is located in the town of Blacksburg in Montgomery County, where a staff of thirty report throughout the year with five more positions filled in the summer.

In my earlier reference to retirement parties, I mentioned optimistic newcomers to the Forest Service workforce and how Dan sympathized with them. In my lengthy interviews with him, he emphatically demonstrated comfort with current policy directions. When I brought up past criticisms such as a preoccupation with timber production, widespread clear-cut harvesting, neglect of wildlife, opposition to a prescribed burning, and disinterest in eco-management, he responded that these shortcomings have largely disappeared with the passage of time. This permits a policy posture that is forward looking but flexible. He identifies himself as diverse in priorities, balanced between perspectives, and occupying a middle ground with respect to conserving the forest in its natural state and disturbing it intelligently.

To illustrate, Dan does not oppose timber sales but insists that they are on appropriate terrain, of limited size, and in accord with long-range species and tree-age goals. Controlled burning is desirable if it is on the right gradient and leads to more tree health but does not damage soils or endanger property. Chain saws and accessible roads must be kept out of wilderness areas, yet primitive camping by small groups can be allowed. Power transmission lines and natural gas pipelines are not welcome but if alternative routes are sought and *no net loss* practices are followed, they may be acceptable. Thus, in general, great forests should be allowed to live out their own natural life cycles, yet in specific instances a light management touch may very well be desirable and indeed essential, to both preserve the ecosystem and serve the greater good. The key to success in such a multiple and cautious approach is always to keep an open mind so as to be prepared to learn from ongoing research.

A second overriding theme in Ranger McKeague's philosophy of work is giving extensive attention to connections with the public. While at one time forest districts were closely associated with small rural communities, subsequent office consolidation led to a less narrow outlook by rangers. One reason for his appointment to the Eastern District was his prior experience with community forestry. Since his arrival, Dan has taken upon himself the task of cultivating connections within the town of Blacksburg and surrounding communities. Joint educational programs have been developed with Virginia Tech's Department of Forest Resources and Environmental Conservation. The lobby of the District's offices on Main Street is made up as "Smokey the Bear's Woods," making it a popular destination for visits by classes of grade school children.

Requirements of the National Environmental Policy Act of 1970 affect most Forest Service projects or program changes. For example, when Dan is preparing to extend or close a Forest Service road, he must either file a Categorical Exclusion that shows the step is environmentally neutral or prepare an Environmental Assessment to assess environmental outcomes and possible alternatives. When this happens, he informally and formally consults with all interested parties, including not only landowners but citizen groups. When a major issue arises such as a new pipeline, the forest supervisor in Roanoke and regional forester in Atlanta become involved. To Dan, the prospect of allowing citizen participation in his decisions is not a matter of debate but of established law.

The District actively promotes citizen volunteerism. Chronic funding short-ages require it throughout the agency, especially in the realm of forest recreation. As in the national parks, volunteers act as campground hosts and trail watchdogs; Dan could not maintain the 150 miles of the Appalachian Trail in the District without consulting its members on needed trail route changes and development.

The third major theme in Ranger McKeague's administration is nurturing the morale and dedication of his employees. He does this with the help of his staff offi-cers that provide professional guidance (without possessing line authority) in the areas of timber management, fire management, recreation, wildlife, roads, and sup-port services. Two of these individuals are female, something that would be unheard of in the male-dominated Forest Service of a few years ago. An all-hands safety meeting is held monthly, sometimes in the field, where current agency issues are discussed, followed on occasion by a potluck lunch. In November 2017, the Eastern District was pronounced the best in the southern region, and to accept the award, Dan took his entire management team to Atlanta for the celebration.

One way Dan identifies himself as a coworker in the District rather than dis-tant head is personal involvement in the Instant Command System used by the Forest Service and most emergency management organizations. It is a standing personnel roster of individuals trained in various aspects of involvement in forest wildfires and comparable events. Each member carries an Incident Qualification Card that stipulates what position he or she is currently qualified to fill on a moment's notice. Dan is qualified as a technical specialist, firefighter Type 2, pub-lic information officer, and agency administrator. During every single fire season, part or most of District personnel are temporarily seconded to emergency work in the field, a vivid experience that draws everyone together more than any social occasions ever could.

As with Izaak Walton's *The Compleat Angler*, Daniel McKeague is The Compleat Common Bureaucrat. He is in his dream job. It involves just the right mix of techni-cal work, leadership, and physical action. He loves to get his Forest Service truck muddy out in the Jefferson National Forest. He is at home in the quiet woods. He is stimulated by the need to motivate his people to do their best for the land. Even though their own labors scatter them across vast terrain, he is determined to keep contact with every man and woman. Interaction with multiple and warring interests is not a problem. He is always prepared to challenge a citizen that wrongs the public's forests, for example, by placing a homemade "Forest Service Road, No Trespassing" sign at the entrance of a private drive. In person, he is warm, informal, and invariably wearing his workaday green uniform without a tie, but always bearing the gold badge. Another Forest Service symbol, his regulation Smokey the Bear Stetson, has long been discarded. Asked whether he will ever leave the organization, the answer is a flat *NO*.

NOTES

1. On the National Park Service, see Goodsell, *Mission Mystique: Belief Systems in Public Agencies* (Washington, DC: CQ Press, 2011), Ch. 2.

2. Forest Supervisor, Tom Speaks. *Press Release*, May 26, 2015.

3. Glen O. Robinson, *The Forest Service* (Baltimore: Johns Hopkins University Press, 1975); William E. Shands and Robert G. Healy, *The Lands Nobody Wanted* (Washington, DC: Conservation Foundation, 1977); Gerald W. Williams, *The USDA Forest Service: The First Century* (Washington, DC: U.S. Forest Service, 2000).

4. Len Shoemaker, *Saga of a Forest Ranger* (Boulder: University of Colorado Press, 1958); Harold K. Steen, *The U.S. Forest Service: A History* (Seattle: University of Washington Press, 1976); Alfred Runte, *Public Lands, Public Heritage: The National Forest Ideal* (Niwot, CO: Roberts Rinehart, 1991).

5. Herbert Kaufman, *The Forest Ranger: A Study in Administrative Behavior* (Baltimore: Johns Hopkins University Press, 1960). Reprint published in 2006 by Resources for the Future.

6. Shands and Healy, 13.

7. U.S. Forest Service website, accessed March 4, 2016.

DANIEL M. RICCIO, Livability Director

A Beautiful Place Kept That Way

Photo by Charles T. Goodsell

We next apply the conservation ethic to the built rather than natural environment. Here, too, good stewardship requires personal care for the resource, consideration for when to intervene, and close interaction with involved citizens.

The City of Charleston, South Carolina, was founded over three centuries ago. It is the home of a rich array of colonial, antebellum, and Victorian private residences and public buildings as well as other notable structures. Their presence has long been a source of pride and beauty to the community. Moreover, Charlestonians are aware of how their port city's commercial, cultural, and recreational assets generally are foremost in the state. Hence, taking good care of the physical manifestations of their beloved city is a matter of high priority.

To help satisfy this need, a novel Livability program has been established by its municipal government. It entails preservation of historic buildings; adequate maintenance of yards, streets, and sidewalks; attaining high standards of refuse collection; traffic and parking management; animal control; and public nuisance mitigation.

The program began by creating, in 2002, what is called the Livability Court. This was done by designating a judge in the municipal criminal court system to be the livability judge and giving that person adjudicatory authority for code enforcement. Over time, informal and flexible ways were developed to handle violations and complaints with minimal use of fines or jail time—although these coercive penalties were available if necessary. The court convenes in a regular trial courtroom in the Municipal Court building each Monday morning at 8:30 sharp and handles on the order of a thousand matters annually.

During its first five years, the court was supported administratively by a single livability supervisor, Dan Riccio. His role was limited to acting as liaison between the court and city departments whose codes needed to be enforced. This arrangement eventually broke down, however, because departments faced with chronic budgetary shortfalls were reluctant to spend scarce resources on a function regarded as secondary in importance. Mr. Riccio had no independent authority to insist that complaints or observed problems be dealt with promptly; hence, case backlogs accumulated and lengthy delays became a major concern.

In response to Mr. Riccio's urging, in 2007 a decision was made to streamline the court's functioning by creating a small bureaucracy that would itself carry out much code enforcement activity in a consolidated and consistent manner. It was named the Livability Division. Following a competitive recruitment search, Dan was named its director. Its staff consisted of professional enforcement officers both transferred from the departments and recruited anew. The office took direct responsibility for (1) independently monitoring existing neighborhood conditions; (2) investigating received citizen complaints across all departmental areas; (3) gathering evidence on potential violations and presenting them to the Livability Court; and (4) ensuring that decisions by the livability judge were carried out.

With a dual set of interlocking adjudicatory and administrative institutions in place, a fully functional Livability program was now possible. As an indicator of its success, when in later years city authorities decided to strengthen tourism regulation within Charleston's historic area, that entire function was assigned to the Livability Division. At the same time, its hierarchical status was raised to that of department; the livability director now sits in the mayor's cabinet under the title Director of Livability and Tourism.

This approach to municipal code enforcement stands as a marked departure from what is traditional in American local government. In most jurisdictions, the enforcement of city codes is decentralized, legalized, marginalized, and punishment-oriented. Employees interested in high-profile programs find such work mechanical and mundane. At budget time, it is an activity that is easy to cut back, leading to chronic neglect of urban physical condition across the country.

Two individuals must be credited for originating the Charleston program. Both are lawyers and native sons of the city. One is Mayor Joseph P. Riley, who at his voluntary retirement from office in 2015 had served as the city's chief executive for forty years by virtue of winning ten elections in a row. Over this time, he revitalized the downtown Historic District, developed a celebrated Waterfront Park, and supported creation of an American version of Italy's Spoleto music festival. In the realm of social policy, Mayor Riley brought to the city added affordable housing, introduced community policing to its police department, created a network of 102 active neighborhood associations, and took repeated leadership steps to reduce racial tensions. It is from this mayor's creative mind alone that the Livability program sprang, although other cities have experimented with special courts for dealing with substance abusers and the mentally disturbed. In Charleston, the tribunal's purpose is not to give special treatment to eligible individuals but to the community as a whole.

The other Livability founder is Judge Michael A. Molony, long a personal friend and political associate of Riley. When the mayor appointed Molony to the municipal criminal bench in 2002, the two men discussed in detail creation of a Livability Court. While Judge Molony did not permanently forgo sitting for general criminal court, he pledged the bulk of his time to this novel judicial venture. The huge backlog of unresolved complaints and citations awaiting municipal adjudication convinced him that the job would be essentially full-time.

Together the two lawyers—one elected to office and the other appointed to the bench—developed a blueprint on how such a court would work. It became the basis for procedures operating up to the present time. After a complaining citizen or enforcement officer identifies a problem, the alleged violator is given a specified time (usually five days) to correct it. If in this time period the problem is not satisfactorily resolved, the Livability Division or City Attorney's Office requests the Livability Court to serve a warrant on the offending party. If granted, a written summons is delivered to the party of concern to appear before the livability judge at a specified date and time. The defendant may obtain counsel, but in the vast majority of cases most legal formalities are suspended. Instead, the accused and the judge simply discuss the matter face-to-face in the open courtroom with the citizen standing before the bench and the judge seated behind it. Typically, Dan or other staff from the Livability Division and pertinent departments is on hand to answer questions.

The precise circumstances of each case are fully considered by the judge without resort to standardized outcomes. If the violation is serious enough, it may earn a fine of up to $1,000 or 30 days in jail, although conferral of such penalties is rare. The general idea is to create a teaching moment in which the problem at hand is quickly solved and the citizen becomes wiser for it. A continuance may be granted to give the offender time to take corrective action, and a pledge in this regard is put in writing with copies sent to affected parties. If the pledge is broken, city employees take action directly and file a lien against the property involved to cover costs.

In these proceedings, normal criminal-law rules are relaxed. Hearsay evidence is admissible. The city assumes the burden of proving guilt, although that finding does not require proof beyond reasonable doubt as in a criminal matter. Judge Molony balances arguments for and against the defendant and decides which is stronger. He maintains an independent posture and does not necessarily decide for the city. If alleged violators are not satisfied with the outcome, they may request a jury trial in which all procedural rights apply and the jury alone determines the facts of the case. Defense counsel may also appeal a city action by challenging the constitutionality of the code in question, and this has happened.

For all this to work, it is essential that the Livability program be supported by the expertise and resources of common bureaucrats. Dan Riccio has led this effort from the beginning. He has been the only director of the Livability Division and is now department head for livability and tourism. Without his day-by-day energy and devotion to the program, it could not have succeeded.

Like Mayor Riley and Judge Molony, Mr. Riccio was born and raised in Charleston. After a hitch in the Army, he obtained a bachelor's degree from Limestone College in Charleston and later earned a master's degree in human resource management at Webster University, also located in the area. Throughout his early years, Dan's career plan was to be a law enforcement officer. He came to this attitude naturally as his father occupied a public safety position at the Charleston naval base for many years. Two brothers also pursued this field.

After attending a state criminal justice academy and working in a public safety job at the Medical University of South Carolina, Mr. Riccio was sworn into the City of Charleston police force. Over a 22-year career, he moved up in rank from private to sergeant and then to lieutenant, during which time he patrolled high-crime areas, broke up gambling rings, and led narcotics investigations among other dangerous assignments. For many years, he was continuously on-call as a member of the SWAT team.

When the Livability Court was originally launched in 2002, Dan was asked by Mayor Riley to take over supervision of the program's liaison relationships with city departments. The thinking was that a veteran policeman was the kind of person who could secure cooperation from citizens as well as department heads. Yet, as efforts to implement the program unfolded, it became clear to Dan that typical police behavior was not going to achieve success. He found himself consciously undergoing a process of self-examination with respect to the attitudes required by the new job. Hence he left his uniform, badge, and gun at home and adopted behavior conducive not to enforcing legal authority but a tolerance for listening and readiness to persuade rather than coerce. Knocking down doors on the SWAT team had to be replaced by educating property owners to show respect for others. By the time Dan retired from the police department to become the Livability Division's permanent civilian head, the transformation was complete.

Nonetheless, Director Riccio's police background had equipped him with traits and habits that became invaluable in performing in this new role. He brought to the job an observant eye, a capacity for absorbing detail, the energy needed for sustained work, and the self-discipline required to sort out problems and set priorities. His reputation for being reliable is legendary. Dan responds to all phone calls and e-mails by day's end, follows complex matters while forgetting nothing, and lives up to all promises if humanly possible. Citizens both powerful and humble that he has dealt with over time are not forgotten. Because of his long service in Charleston's government, he knows key people in all departments. As a result, this common bureaucrat was and still is *the* person to go to in Charleston's bureaucracy to get something done.

At the same time, this tightly wound official does not fall victim to the classic bureaucratic disease of worshiping the sanctity of the rules for their own sake at the expense of ignoring their intended purpose. The thick volume of codes adopted by Charleston's city fathers over the years is scrupulously followed, albeit sometimes in spirit rather than literally. Dan sees the role of code enforcer not being that of demanding total compliance but rather discovering ways to apply code provisions to concrete situations in a timely and sensible way. When asked what general principle guides this norm of action, Dan cites what he calls the Golden Rule of bureaucracy: treat citizens as you would wish to be treated as a citizen. Hence, he *always* takes queries seriously and *always* reports back on what could be done and what could not be done and *why*—all fully explained.

Director Riccio makes a point of imbuing all members of his staff with these precepts and values. Like their leader, these thirteen men and women present themselves to the public as ordinary civilian bureaucrats. They wear no badge or sign of rank and are not armed. The only "uniform" is a blue knit T-shirt bearing the legend Livability Division. When on duty, they travel in unmarked city cars or their own vehicles. Communication with the home office is by car radio or cell phone. They keep in close touch with each other as well and share office space in two nearby buildings. To transport heavy files back and forth, the Division sports a top-of-the-line child's play wagon bearing the word Livability.

Staff members are assigned to teams and duties that are defined by the division's mission of holistic livability promotion, including preference for persuasion over coercion. This is an important point because it implicitly rejects the pre-2007 fragmented arrangement whereby individual departments controlled enforcement on their own terms in their own jurisdictions.

Four officers are assigned to what is called the Residential Code Enforcement Team. This "environmental" work, as they call it, consists of dealing with lawns out of control, foliage overgrowth, excessive litter, derelict vehicles, the accumulation or dumped debris, and trash cans left untended. In addition, the team responds to animal violations, noise nuisances, and underage drinking.

Director Riccio developed a regional approach to environmental enforcement whereby each of the four team members is responsible for a separate territory. This is essential because Metro Charleston includes not merely the historic downtown area but numerous remote peninsulas and islands. This is what the police department was doing when Dan served in it, and he incorporated a similar arrangement for his division.

In addition, Dan emulated police practice by keying into regional administration of Charleston's 102 active neighborhood associations. Each association regularly invites its members to attend a monthly evening meeting, chaired by that group's elected president. The city assigns an individual police officer to each association in order to be available to attend if needed to solve crime problems. Dan arranges for a similar practice by members of the enforcement team. That person accepts an invitation to come to the meeting when asked to suggest ways to improve the appearance of the local landscape and encourage sensible neighborhood practices. Dan himself occasionally appears to explain the role of the Livability Division and Court.

Orderly environmental presentation is especially important to Charleston's historic areas where tourists roam. Accordingly, the central business district is treated as a fifth code enforcement area to which a single livability officer is assigned full-time. Of special concern downtown is storefront neatness, unimpeded sidewalks, and prompt garbage disposal. In addition, this officer deals with zoning regulations, business licenses, parking lot appeals, peddlers, solicitors for charitable causes, and craft artisans selling their wares.

Another team addresses a problem peculiar to historic residential housing located in low-income neighborhoods. It is called the Substandard Housing Team, composed of three officers. Its members monitor the condition of vacant residential and business structures that are in danger of progressive deterioration, collapse, or occupation by vagrants or stray animals. All such buildings must meet the minimum standards for eventual historic property preservation. These are to be boarded up and made watertight; kept free of surrounding litter, overgrowth, and debris; and posted with No Trespassing signs.

The vacant structures team is led by Shannon E. Tilman. Another Charleston native, Ms. Tilman had previously served as administrative assistant for code enforcement with the city police. During the Livability Division's early years, she acquired experience with environmental enforcement. When the mayor and Dan decided more attention should be given to vacant structures, she was given the title of building compliance coordinator and headed the Substandard Housing Team.

At this writing, Shannon supervises the continuous physical monitoring of some 400 structures, covering about 150 by herself. She drives by them daily to determine whether a boarded-up door has been pried open or a porch roof is falling down. When something is amiss, a crew is immediately called in for repairs or installation of temporary supports. If trespassing homeless persons are detected inside the building, the police are called; the individuals are coaxed out without being arrested and delivered to the appropriate social services entity for treatment and care.

Absentee landlords that allow their properties to deteriorate flagrantly are not treated so gently. They are hunted down if possible and ordered to appear before the Livability Court. It is this aspect of her work that she likes least; the one she likes best is when an investor or preservation group becomes interested in saving an abandoned property and proceeds to renovate or rebuild it for adaptive reuse. Along this line, Shannon is particularly pleased that the disintegrating home of her grandfather on Queen Street—known as the Graham House—is now a fashionable restaurant.

Two other units of the Livability Division deserve mention. One is the Quick Response Squad, composed of two officers. Their activities include removing graffiti as soon as it is encountered; tearing down private notices placed in public places ("snipe signage"); hauling away abandoned locked bicycles; and boarding up windows spotted by the Substandard Housing Team.

The second unit sponsors the Keep Charleston Beautiful volunteer program, one of more than 600 affiliates of the national Keep America Beautiful organization. This is a nonprofit organization founded in 1953 to promote urban litter removal, recycling bins, and planting projects. An emphasis in Charleston's program is to recruit college students and corporate employees to pick up trash along highways and under bridges. Also a spring "Move Out Day" is held to remove old furniture and other unwanted items from the street that have been left behind by departing college students.

In sum, the traditionally mundane local government function of code enforcement has been redefined in Charleston as a novel and attention-getting venture. The city's rich architectural heritage, booming port and tourism economies, and endowment of well-known cultural and education institutions are seen as deserving the highest possible quality of building physicality and street conditions. As we have seen, the Livability program seeks to achieve this end not by draconian rule but by a continuous process of reasoned discussion, individualized action, and mutual respect.

Three personalities in the municipal government made this happen. Each represents a different arm of that government. Mayor Joseph Riley, the elected mayor for four decades, had the wisdom, insight, and creativity to give birth to the idea and attach to it the Livability name. His reputation and influence made it possible to take this idea and run with it by mobilizing the necessary political and institutional support. This was done, remarkably, without new legislation and with minimal added funding. He continued to shepherd the program through its developmental years, during which it was significantly reorganized.

The second individual is Judge James Molony. He joined with the mayor in developing the Livability Court's relatively informal legal procedures, bringing to fruition a system capable of processing a thousand or more cases annually in a timely manner. His contribution has caught the attention of the legal community, and the court has become a model for other cities to adopt, particularly in South Carolina.

Along with the mayor's political contribution and the judge's legal one, Dan Riccio has provided the program's administrative grounding. Without his leadership, implementation of the program would never have got off the ground. By its nature, successful code enforcement requires scrupulous attention to detail, constant interaction with multiple parties, and a reputation for reliability that makes possible the building of citizen trust. The inner transformation Dan made when moving from the police department to the Livability Division could be said to be the key to its administrative success; a 180-degree turn from chasing criminals to mediating disputes cannot but help sharpen the realization of what *not* to do in directing this unique organization.

Looked at in its totality, one might also argue that the Charleston Livability program represents in microcosm the proper posture that public administration as a whole should assume in the local setting. What Mr. Riccio has done in his conduct is not to become preoccupied with the smoothness of internal operations alone. The standard issues of public management—efficiency, cost reduction, and productivity—are of secondary importance to him. What really counts is how well the program is maximizing the physical attractiveness of the city in an atmosphere of personal cooperation. To generalize this notion, the state of the local government itself is of secondary importance to the state of the community for which it labors. In the case of the Livability enterprise, a good community is one in which residents are conscious of the quality of their physical surroundings because of the pride they have in the place where they live. This is precisely the kind of purpose that can elevate public administration to an exalted level in a democratic society.

KEITH T. GRUPPOSO, Probation Officer
Giving Second Chances When Possible

Photo by Charles T. Goodsell

So far, our essays on Public Conservation have dealt with the natural and then urban environment. This essay deals with what might be thought of as the human environment. By this I mean giving second chances to juveniles on their way to going astray. What is being conserved is part of the lifeblood of the nation.

Some 175 years ago, two social inventions emerged in criminal law at almost the same time, thousands of miles apart. Both liberalized the accepted doctrine of autocracies and democracies alike that convicted criminals are to be punished in full. One of these is *parole*, a conditioned reprieve from sentence duration and/or follow-through monitoring. It began when Alexander Maconochie, warden of an English penal colony in the South Pacific, established a "mark system" of incentives whereby inmates could earn early release for good behavior.[1]

The second invention is *probation*, an alternative to incarceration that seeks justice by more productive means. Its inventor was Boston industrialist John Augustus, who initiated a practice of personally posting bail for drunkards heading for jail under the proposition that a shot at rehabilitation might convince the judge to impose a fine.[2]

It is these two revolutionary concepts in the criminal justice field that underlie the public service rendered by Keith T. Grupposo, a juvenile probation officer in Fairfax County, Virginia. This jurisdiction, situated to the west of the District of Columbia, is the second wealthiest county in the United States in terms of median household income. At the same time, its million-plus population is highly varied; no less than a third of its residents speak at home a language other than English.

Another notable feature of Fairfax County is that its government does not have jurisdiction over all 395 square miles of its territory. The cities of Falls Church, Alexandria, and Fairfax City within it are independent. Yet Fairfax City is regarded as the Fairfax County seat, an anomaly made possible by construing the land on which the county's Government Center and Judicial Center stand to be county enclaves.

The Judicial Center is a large complex of several structures including old and new courthouses, old and new jails, court clerk offices, and a juvenile detention center. The oldest courthouse in the complex dates from 1800 and is today used for assistance to crime victims. It was in its restored courtroom that the video accompanying this essay was filmed.

Three active courts operate at the Judicial Center. The State Circuit Court for the 19th Circuit is the court of original jurisdiction for all serious crimes and major civil litigation. With fourteen judges, it is the largest trial court in the Commonwealth. A second judicial body is the General District Court, a local court that adjudicates minor crimes, misdemeanors, ordinance violations, traffic infractions, and lesser civil cases. Its ten judges hear cases as well in the towns of Herndon and Vienna, Virginia.

The Judicial Center's third court is the Juvenile and Domestic Relations District Court. Its jurisdiction includes Fairfax County, the City of Fairfax, and the towns of Herndon, Vienna, and Clifton. As the name implies, the court's work deals with two separate but often interrelated realms: (1) offenses on the part of juveniles and (2) family matters experienced by adults alone. Its judicial roster contains eight positions but only seven are currently filled. Their collective work-load is heavy: an average of 200 or more docketed transactions are dealt with every session day, adding up to some 30,000 hearings annually for juveniles and 25,000 for adults.[3]

As with the other courts, Juvenile-Domestic judges are appointed by the Virginia General Assembly for fixed terms and compensated by the state. Clerks and immediate court personnel under them are also state employees. Unlike the circuit and district tribunals, the proceedings of the Juvenile and Domestic Relations court are before a judge only rather than jury and are closed to the general public.

This court is exceptional in another major way. With it is associated a full-fledged bureaucracy supervised and funded by the county and not the state. Its name is the Court Services Unit (CSU), and it is where Mr. Grupposo is employed. Hence, Keith is a local government employee whose duties are in behalf of the local judiciary. However, his employer is an executive agency in all other respects. The Court Services Unit reports to the county executive and is thereby responsible to the County Board. It is a sizable entity of 300 employees with a budget of $21 million. All standard bureaucratic properties are present, such as specialization, hierarchy, a catchment area, and geographic field offices—known as the North, South, East, and Central CSU offices.

The organization develops its own procedures, does its own hiring, maintains its own records, independently engages with partners and undergoes program evaluation and auditing. In other Virginia jurisdictions, judicial bureaucracies exist, but typically only to conduct court business. In the Fairfax case, common bureaucrats of local government are deeply involved in actually deciding cases.

Keith was born and raised in Bellingham, Massachusetts, and grew up in a family of three sons. His parents were intensely sports-minded and encouraged their boys to play baseball and football on school and community teams. Keith's father, Kevin, coached community teams and his mother, Mary Louise, actively participated in game life.

When it came time for college, Keith migrated south to Virginia to attend Marymount University in Arlington County, also near the District of Columbia. He majored in psychology with an applied emphasis on human service delivery. One day, a corrections worker visited a class he was taking and spoke on the subject of helping prisoners reenter society. Keith immediately took an interest in her kind of work, but from his family experience of participating in boyhood sports, he wanted to help juveniles, not adults.

For an internship to complete his degree program, Keith selected a semester in which he counseled adults under detention in both Arlington and Fairfax Counties. Upon graduating in 2005, he sought and accepted a job as Probation

Counselor I with the Fairfax CSU Juvenile Detention Center. This facility is, despite its name, a sizable jail located within the Judicial Center. Its footprint consists of a hollow square with central open courtyard surrounded by eleven living areas. Each one contains eleven bedrooms, creating a bed capacity of 121. Glass walls separate most internal spaces to reduce resident anxiety and enable staff surveillance. The design permits a small-group feel yet allows segregation by gang membership and gender, with boys far more common than girls. A Maconochie-style behavioral point system is used to encourage obedience.

After two years at the Detention Center, Keith was reassigned to another highly disciplined CSU program known as Supervised Release Services. In it, juveniles no longer needing detention are released to the care of family members in a modified form of house arrest. They may leave home only to attend school, go to work and accompany a parent, while staying clear of drugs and respecting a curfew. GPS ankle bracelets check on their location to enforce these rules.

Then in 2010, five years after being initially hired, Mr. Grupposo was promoted to Probation Counselor II. The advance meant a transfer from the Judicial Center in Fairfax City to the North CSU office in Reston, where he still works. Keith now had the status of journeyman probation officer entitled to handle the intake of juveniles who had come to police attention, administer risk assessment tests on them, monitor their compliance to rules, and manage wrap-around services for a return to society.

In this job, he had the opportunity to become familiar with other CSU probation programs. Examples are the Boy's Probation House for youngsters ages 14 to 17, the Transitional Living Program for 18- to 19-year-olds, and Foundations, a treatment cottage for delinquent girls. Juveniles who enter the system as runaways or truants are directed to Shelter II, a short-term residential experience run with a lighter touch. In cooperation with the Department of Corrections, a parole process operates for sentenced juveniles upon conclusion of their sentences.

Keith's job takes on ceremonial public character when he testifies at judicial hearings. These occur in one of the seven identical courtrooms in active use. The probation officer sits at a desk facing the high judicial bench, just below the judge, who looks out to the parties and audience. In accord with custom, the defense table is situated at floor level to the judge's right and the prosecution table to his or her left. This seating arrangement places defense counsel (with his or her client), the probation officer, and the state's attorney on a level plane but with Keith occupying the central position, in closest proximity to the elevated judge.

As the proceedings unfold, the judge informs the offender of his or her rights and then has Keith present a statement on the background of the case and his recommendations for its resolution. Attorneys representing the two sides present their positions relative to the plan Keith has already put forward. After subsequent questioning, the judge enters his or her decision, often aligned with Keith's proposal. In short, the probation officer's standing and influence are preeminent in the hearing situation, both symbolically and behaviorally. Here, the public administrator does not merely follow legal decisions, he or she shapes them.

The next promotion for our rising young probation officer came in 2015. In addition to continuing to perform his program duties, Mr. Grupposo now bears the title of assistant director of unit activities at the North office. This means generally supervising the daily work of a staff of eight as well as standing in for the director when she is absent. In this capacity, he assigns new cases to counselors, reviews notes from ongoing cases, examines future client service plans, and hires new staff when needed.

Yet, despite being elevated to management, Keith has never lessened his preoccupation with operations. He is definitely pleased with the work he has been doing these past eleven years. Each day is different and he is eager to get to the office each morning. The sense of purpose that pervades his thinking echoes the "second chance" moral philosophy of John Augustus—do what is possible to turn around lives that possess a future potential while protecting the public's safety.

In retrospect, Keith's early assignments in detention and protection had convinced him that subjecting juveniles not at risk to the indignities of house arrest or throwing them in jail alongside members of the MS-13 criminal gang is wrong for impulsive but salvageable boys and girls. It can do little but encourage deeper alienation and more hardened criminality. Now that he has administrative responsibilities, Keith has the opportunity to pass on such sentiments to others. In so doing, he is not acting alone but in accord with waves of change already sweeping through the CSU organization.

A specific goal that has become particularly important in Keith's mind is to screen effectively those juveniles who come to police attention in order to make wise decisions on their disposition. This must be done on an objective basis, although informed hunches help. Should they be sent through normal legal channels where they would be stuck with a criminal record and sentenced to house arrest or jail? Or would they best be diverted to non-court options that might lead to rehabilitation and deserving a second chance? How can this high-stakes decision be made quickly, on the spot, by busy intake officers?

The answer is a set of two assessment measures. One of these is the Youth Assessment and Screening Instrument (YASI). It measures risk of doing more harm by generating scores in ten different domains, and from these factors produce a rating on a six-point scale with low being more favorable. When fully employed, the software develops a narrative report that summarizes findings and produces a draft social history that can be used by the probation officer in court.

A second test is the Global Appraisal of Individual Needs Short Screener (GAIN-SS), which takes only five minutes to administer. It utilizes a series of questions that begin with the phrase, "When was the last time that you . . . ?" followed by such conditions as felt depressed, considered suicide, started a fight, had shaky hands from drug use, or grabbed or shoved someone.

Fairfax intake officers examine results from a condensed version of YASI and GAIN-SS and then place held juveniles into one of three categories: low risk, moderate risk, and high risk. Those falling into the first category are presented with the possibility of being released with no court appearance if they and their families agree to a period of up to 90 days of professional counseling, other behavior health treatment, and possibly a substance abuse program if necessary. If, at the end of this period, signs of disruptive or unlawful behavior are still occurring, the subject's status is up for reconsideration.

Those classified as moderate risk are dealt with in one of two ways. One option is a nonjudicial hearing before a CSU hearing officer in which the circumstances, intentions, and motives behind the offense are explored informally, in the company of family and others. Following this meeting, the hearing officer imposes a condition for release such as a period of 90 days in community service.

The second option is monitored diversion, which consists of imposing enumerated conditions and regular meetings with a diversion counselor for up to 90 days. If the juvenile is assessed at high risk, he or she automatically undergoes the monitored diversion option, which includes wearing a GPS ankle bracelet. As in the other options, unacceptable behavior after the trial period means start-over reconsideration.

Although the most recent data are not available, figures up to 2013 indicate that the diversion policy has had a significant effect on keeping delinquents out of the court system. The total number of yearly juvenile court hearings dropped from 33,939 in Calendar Year 2009 to 29,767 in Calendar Year 2013, a decline of 12 percent. A downstream consequence of this lessened intake activity has been to reduce the number of court-ordered probation cases even more: from 774 in Fiscal Year 2009 to 510 in Fiscal Year 2013, a 34 percent drop. Likewise, numbers of initiated community service assignments declined from 2,210 to 1,110, or 50 percent. Perhaps most satisfying, the typical daily population at the Juvenile Detention Center is now about 25, compared to 100 or so a few years back.[4]

When I asked Keith what his future career plans are, he responded that he is pleased where he is and looks forward to being associated with the organization for the foreseeable future. He has no plans to seek another position or higher salary elsewhere. After all, he points out, the Fairfax juvenile program is the largest of its kind in the state and is on the leading edge of change nationwide. Its internal goal is to become the best in the country.

To support such optimism, Keith points out how Fairfax is a leader not only in intake diversion but in other areas of reform as well. There are several, and I limit myself to three.[5]

One is attempts to diminish the disproportionate number of minority juveniles entering and remaining in its programs. A Structured Decision Making model was developed whereby case managers consciously search for opportunities in the full range of client processing where minority contact can be reduced. In cooperation with Fairfax public schools, social services, and the police, a study was funded to search for underlying causes of the problem.

Another segment of the client population needing special attention is girls. After study, it has been realized that troubled girls face different problems than boys. In the first place, their offenses tend to be less serious, which leads to a downplaying of problems and hence services. Second, the effects of trauma are different between the genders. Sexual abuse exerts a more lasting effect on young women. When frightened or angry, girls tend to react not with lashing out but striking within, leading to depression. In order to increase sensitivity within the staff to these gender differences, an informal group called the Girls Circle has been formed among their counselors.

A third example of change has been to discourage accusatory questioning of offending juveniles, as the police typically do with adult suspects. Keith favors using open-ended questions so the adolescents can tell their own stories unimpeded. An allied movement called Motivational Interviewing takes the next step by eliciting and exploring—in an atmosphere of acceptance and compassion—the young person's own reasons for seeking to make big changes in his or her life.

A final example of forward movement is to bring families more fully into the development of their own sons and daughters. This is a goal of particular interest to Keith. He has expressed himself eloquently on the matter, and I pass on his thoughts directly.

> What I hope is that the Court Service Unit continues to find new ways to work with our clients and to encourage solutions on a community level. Over the past year, we have put a lot of work into keeping low-risk, first-time offenders out of the court system. However, we do so while making sure to discuss needs and risk factors that are highlighted by our assessments. We provide referrals to services to families and put responsibility on the individual, parents, and families as a whole with the hope of empowering them to address their own needs. I have found helping families in this way to be rewarding and feel that many families have come into meetings worrying about "what the court will do to them," but have left feeling that we worked as a team to come up with a plan to address the issue. My hope is that we will find more opportunities for this type of intervention to promote self-sufficiency that empowers families.[6]

To conclude, we have here a sincere young public servant whose attributes include authentic belief in a mission that is crucial yet mostly hidden from public view; personal competence in carrying out one's work; ongoing desire to strive for better results; doing so as a loyal organization member and not lone wolf; and helping citizens to take responsibility for bettering their own lives.

NOTES

1. Joan Petersilia, "Parole and Prisoner Reentry in the United States," *Crime and Justice* 26 (Chicago: University of Chicago Press, 1999): 487–488.

2. Joan Petersilia, "Probation in the United States," *Crime and Justice* 25 (Chicago, University of Chicago Press, 1998): 32–33.

3. Court Service Unit of the Fairfax County Juvenile and Domestic Relations District Court, Annual Statistical Report for FY 2003–2004, 4; Court Service Unit of the Fairfax County Juvenile and Domestic Relations District Court, Annual Statistical Report for FY 2009–2013, 20.

4. Court Service Unit of the Fairfax County Juvenile and Domestic Relations District Court, Annual Statistical Report for FY 2009–2013, 20, 32, 34.

5. In the following examples of change, I draw not only on Mr. Grupposo's insights but on commentary in the Annual Statistical Report for FY 2009–2013, 12–14.

6. E-mail from subject to author dated January 10, 2017.

PART FOUR

PUBLIC WELL-BEING

KATHY D. ROBERTSON, Homelessness Combatant

Making Homeless Programs Work

Photo by Charles T. Goodsell

This last category of essays, Public Well-Being, is broader than previous ones. Its advantage is that while being totally compatible with what public administration is all about, it also accommodates our last trio of common bureaucrats whose work areas are very different. All pursue citizen well-being, but in different degrees of subject-matter focus. We start with an individual whose purpose is sharply defined, that of redeeming the homeless and ending the problem in Virginia.

For decades, homelessness was not very visible as a problem in America. In the city environment, drifters got a bed and meal at the local storefront mission. In rural areas, they gathered as hoboes around a campfire near the railroad tracks. In the 1970s and 1980s, however, the phenomenon—defined generally as persons without regular and adequate nighttime residence—grew exponentially. The reasons cannot be known with certainty, but possibilities are gentrification of urban skid rows, reluctance of families to take in undesirable kin, decriminalization of vagrancy and drunkenness, and higher admission standards at mental hospitals.[1]

A growth in the number of homeless families was particularly apparent in Los Angeles. In 1988, local activist Tanya Tull formed a nonprofit called Beyond Shelter. Its purpose was to ameliorate the problem by overcoming barriers to the rental market such as poor credit or prior evictions. Later, Tull changed strategy and adopted what she called "Housing First." The idea was to move families quickly into a stable living space so they could receive home-based services from external providers. In 2012, her organization merged with another California nonprofit, People Assisting the Homeless (PATH). Its mission was to construct new long-term sheltering facilities for both families and individuals. The united group is today called PATH Beyond Shelter.[2]

The Housing First idea was elaborated upon by a Columbia University professor of psychiatry, Sam Tsemberis. In 1992, he formed the group Pathways for Housing, which eventually attracted millions of dollars in city and federal grants and processed some 3,000 homeless people in New York City and elsewhere along the Eastern Seaboard. His contribution was to try to overcome mental health problems and alcohol/drug addiction as a way of reducing homelessness. The effort is based on five principles: (1) immediate housing placement with no readiness conditions; (2) free choice on when to start and when to stop participation; (3) a stated goal of recovery from the malady experienced; (4) individualized, person-driven support systems; and (5) social integration into the community. Tsemberis claims 85 percent success in rehabilitating the homeless.[3]

The federal government entered this arena in force in 1997, with passage of the McKinney-Vento Homeless Assistance Act, the statutory granddaddy of today's federal homelessness programs. Its name memorializes two congressmen who worked tirelessly on getting the legislation passed. In 2009, Congress followed up with the HEARTH Act, standing for Homeless Emergency Assistance and Rapid Transition to Housing. Essentially, it reauthorized existing programs while increasing degrees of flexibility needed for the housing first paradigm.[4]

Today, no less than seven federal departments administer homeless programs. In five instances, they serve this need as an offshoot of their own different mission.

The Department of Education makes homeless grants to state departments of education who in turn distribute funds to school districts to ensure children in this category attend school. The Department of Homeland Security funnels money to FEMA to help victims of natural disasters whose homes have been destroyed. The Department of Justice offers aid to victims of crime who have lost their homes. Veterans Affairs operates several grants and directly administered programs to aid homeless veterans. The Labor Department also assists returning veterans and those exiting hospitals that want to reenter the workforce but cannot afford a place to live.

For two key federal departments, homelessness is integral to their own mission. Health and Human Services (HHS) administers three grant programs, one for outpatient health centers, a second to provide "wrap-around" social services of various kinds, and a third formula-driven fund distribution to states for mental health treatment or drug detoxification. Also, a runaway youth program is administered directly by an HHS bureau. Together, these activities were appropriated $594 million in FY 2015.

Housing and Urban Development (HUD) spends more than any department in this policy domain. In FY 2015, its Homeless Assistance program was appropriated $2.1 billion for Homeless Assistance grants. These have been in existence since 1987, and they have gone through a number of permutations; at present, they are flexibly designed to support a housing first approach to homeless intervention. Another HUD activity is a formula fund distribution program to entitlement areas for the Emergency Solutions grant that permits wide latitude on the money's use in urban areas. Less populated places are covered by state-allocated grants, which in turn are distributed to local governments and community agencies.

Passage of the HEARTH Act in 2009, and the attention it aroused in the process, stimulated new levels of homeless action around the country among advocacy groups and officials. This happened to a high degree in Virginia. In April 2010, Governor Bob McDonnell issued Executive Order 10 calling for a housing policy framework with a focus on homelessness. Indeed, he set a concrete goal with respect to the latter, that of decreasing the problem by 15 percent by the end of his term in office.

As a result, a Homeless Outcomes Advisory Committee was established for Virginia to work out strategies of reaching that goal. It was co-chaired by Dr. William Hazel Jr., secretary of health and human resources, and Bob Sledd, senior economic advisor. The committee, consisting of state agencies and statewide representation from what are called "continua of care" and homeless service providers, met intensely for several months and developed a plan recommending five specific strategies. As administrator of state and federal funding on the subject, the Department of Housing and Community Development (DHCD) led by William C. Shelton (now retired) was instrumental in implementing the plan. It is at this point in our essay that Ms. Kathy D. Robertson steps into the picture.

A true Virginian, Ms. Robertson was born and raised in Chesterfield County near Richmond and received a bachelor's degree in psychology from the University of Virginia. After college, she worked in several social work positions in Richmond. Five years later, she turned to the private sector and became employed by Financial Insurance Consultants, a Richmond-based insurance and investment company, eventually rising to the position of assistant brokerage manager.

In 1988, Ms. Robertson took yet another cross-sector plunge and joined for its launch the Virginia Lottery, a quasi-governmental revenue-raising entity. Remaining in the lottery industry for 12 years, she worked first as a sales training coordinator and later for a private vendor as director of lottery operations, training, and marketing.

In 2000, this flexible-career professional shifted from organizational employment to singly carrying out training and project management tasks using the leadership skills she had accumulated. This led to part-time work at the Virginia Department of Housing and Community Development. In 2006, she was offered a full-time job in the Department's Homeless and Special Housing unit within its Housing Division, a position she accepted with pleasure and still occupies.

Behind this satisfaction was a major change of heart then going on inside Kathy. This was to shift from enjoying successive, interesting economic opportunities to making a lasting commitment to the public good—"to make a difference," in her words. Looking back, her parents, Jim and Vera Robertson, had always stressed to Kathy and her sister and brother the importance of being humble, kind, and generous in life. Kathy was now ready to honor these sentiments professionally. What greater difference could be made than to give homeless Virginians a chance for a new life?

Getting the new Homeless Outcomes Advisory Committee up and running gave Kathy an opportunity to be on the ground floor of McDonnell's drive to reduce Virginia's homeless population. She, along with Shea Hollifield, then deputy director of Housing at DHCD, and Generra Peck of the Office of Secretary for Commerce and Trade, served as the committee's staff. From this experience Kathy was privileged to become acquainted with all the players in this policy domain and also to appreciate the nuances of what each group visualized as desirable and possible.

Her second introductory opportunity came when a Governor's Coordinating Council on Homeless was created to implement the strategies coming out of the Outcomes Advisory Committee. It was co-chaired by Hazel and Sledd and made up of a cross-section of state and local officials and nonprofit leaders. Similar to the U.S. Interagency Council on Homelessness in Washington, its charge was to achieve the degree of collaboration across state and local governments and public-private sectors to ensure that the needed interaction is achieved to succeed. The Council met quarterly and formed four committees and numerous ad hoc working groups to work out the details. As an emerging key figure in the Housing First area, Kathy served regularly on all bodies. She also co-chaired the Council's Interagency Partnership to Prevent and End Youth Homelessness.

Ms. Robertson is a key official in DHCD's Division of Housing, directed by Pam Kestner. As the head of one of the Division's subunits, Homeless and Special

Needs Housing, she was given the title of associate director for Homeless and Special Needs Housing. This unit boasts a staff of six. Nichele Carver, as Housing Program administration manager, supervises a team of three persons often in the field, namely Kendall Cloeter, Monica Spradin, and Aaron Shoemaker. Reporting directly to Kathy are two more staff, Violet Peyton, Housing Program analyst, and Andriea Ukrop, continuum of care coordinator.

I turn now to the strategies that Ms. Robertson and her crew and colleagues used to transform the homeless services delivery system in Virginia. Officially, a homeless person is defined by HUD as "an individual who lacks a fixed, regular, and adequate nighttime residence," with various elaborations depending on the federal program. As of January 2017, 553,742 such persons existed in the United States, with 6,067 in Virginia.[5]

One key tactic the housing first doctrine uses to combat this intolerable situation is called Rapid Rehousing. This refers to the quick, emergency-response action of placing previously unnoticed homeless persons or families in a stable place to live. This step is seen as absolutely essential to helping them. The reasoning behind this tactic is that only this way can professional and medical attention be applied adequately to have any value. Even if the person is safely housed for the moment in a shelter somewhere, it is impossible to mobilize the community's available support services to aid a single isolated case on a one-time basis. In addition, having a fixed home gives the affected individual or family a sense of security and a self-concept of personal standing that is otherwise unachievable.

Kathy and her colleagues realized full well that the only way to achieve system transformation was to enlist the help of virtually every community in the state. This is done by means of a concept that was already in place called Continuum of Care (CoC). This composite group, composed of all kinds of service providers both public and private, is given responsibility to locate and manage an effective set of intervention activities within its geographic place. A distinction is made between two kinds of CoCs, using somewhat clumsy language: Continua of Care are organized as self-standing performing units while Balance of State Continuum of Care groups are decentralized with disparate components. In Virginia, fifteen of the first type have been formed, coupled with one of the second type consisting of twelve local planning groups. In both types, the CoC develops and operates its collaborative activity independently, albeit doing so in compliance with guidelines. Also, it is accountable for expenditure of received funds. For students of public administration, this unusual arrangement constitutes a remarkable example of participatory collaborative action within the framework of federalism.

Early in the transformation of homeless services in Virginia, the Freddie Mac Foundation caught wind of the homeless plan in the Commonwealth and wanted to contribute to its efforts. The stars seemed magically aligned at this moment for facilitating big change. Three partners cooperated in taking advantage of the Foundation's generosity. These were the Commonwealth of Virginia, National Alliance to End Homelessness, and Virginia Coalition to End Homelessness (later renamed Virginia Housing Alliance). The funded initiative they received was called "Reducing Family Homelessness in Virginia: A Rapid Rehousing Approach." What it set in motion was a beneficial way to shift resources around flexibly and simultaneously build capacity of grantees to act toward shifting to a housing first model. Special help provided by the National Alliance was to sponsor and conduct training sessions for everyone involved. Cooperative learning events were organized around the state whereby CoC participants learned from each other's experiences at change. At one point a 100-Day Challenge was held that yielded the rapid rehousing of 545 families over this time.[6]

Another step taken was to expand the number of what are called Permanent Supportive Housing units. These are living units for those needing more in-depth services, often the chronically homeless. Ideally located in the resident's own community, they are set up so that local provider groups and volunteers are available to provide continuous wrap-around services as needed. Aside from the moral dimension, permanent supportive housing possesses economic advantages as well: it is far less costly on a per-day basis than emergency rooms, hospital stays, or incarceration in jail. By 2013, some 2,164 more beds were added to Virginia's inventory.[7]

In retrospect, how well did housing first work in Virginia? The question can be addressed quantitatively. For several years, HUD has employed annual point-in-time estimates of the number of homeless individuals and families in the country during a single 24-hour period occurring the last week of January. This is done by CoC personnel and trained volunteers who search their territory for persons who are sleeping outside or huddled in such places as cars or under bridges. Current law also defines homelessness as being in emergency shelters or transitional housing. This "sheltered" calculation count is made via electronic records and is kept statistically distinct from "unsheltered" persons who are alone outside. This methodology is by no means flawless but is the best available and a sound indicator of trends.[8]

As noted, Governor McDonnell called for a 15 percent decrease in homelessness in Virginia by the end of his term in January 2014. Kathy and her staff were sweating bullets over reaching that goal at the last minute, and were relieved to discover the number had reached 16 percent. During the next governor's administration, that of Democrat Terry McAuliffe (2014–2018), making progress on homelessness continued. Point-in-time data from 2010 to 2017 showed a drop of total homeless persons from 9,080 to 6,027, or 33.6 percent. For households with adults and children, the decline was 46.5 percent. Decreases of 42.7 percent occurred for chronic homeless individuals, 55.5 percent for chronically homeless people in families, 62 percent for chronic substance abuse cases, and 24.7 percent for persons suffering serious mental illness.[9]

Governor McAuliffe took particular interest in the fate of homeless veterans. Responding to a campaign initiated by Michelle Obama, in 2014, he joined thirteen mayors in the eastern region of the state to sponsor a leave-the-streets "boot camp" and 100-Day Challenge. It succeeded in removing 462 veterans from a homeless situation. On a statewide basis, between 2011 and 2017 the number of home-less veterans dropped from 931 to 478. In 2015, the U.S. Interagency Council on Homelessness declared Virginia as the first state in the union to end veteran home-lessness "functionally"—meaning specific criteria were met and there is a system in place that ensures homelessness is rare, brief, and nonrecurring.[10]

Ms. Kathy D. Robertson does not, of course, deserve all the credit for this rare example of tangible public success in mitigating a stubborn and difficult social prob-lem. The achievement involved countless others in and out of state government and has taken place in some other states as well. Yet we should remember that all too often seemingly perfect "big ideas" for mass social change in our democracy are disappointing when it comes to outcomes. This one, however, is working.

Kathy's contribution to bringing this big idea to Virginia was absolutely essen-tial. Her labors as a common bureaucrat who came to public service late have been tireless, diligent, and indispensable in the handling of detail. Without this steadfast combatant to keep the program alive, continuously probing for ways to improve it and stay true to its values, the Virginia homeless program could easily have become old hat, unexciting, and barely noticed.

NOTES

1. Congressional Research Service, *Homelessness: Targeted Federal Programs and Recent Legislation* (Washington, DC: Author, May 6, 2015).

2. Websites of both organizations, accessed June 14, 2017.

3. Tsemberis has published a manual on his model: *Housing First*, rev. ed. (Center City, MN: Hazelden, 2015). See Wikipedia articles "Pathways to Housing" and "Sam Tsemberis," retrieved online June 14, 2017.

4. Information on these laws and the following federal programs taken from Congressional Research Service, *Homelessness*, 5, 7–19, 26.

5. U.S. Department of Housing and Urban Development, Office of Community Planning and Development, *The 2017 Annual Homeless Assessment Report (AHAR) to Congress* (Washington, DC: Author, December 2017). This definition, used for years in the McKinney-Vento Act, has been amended by the HEARTH Act and varies by federal program.

6. Pamela Kestner and Kathy Robertson, "How Virginia Uses Collaboration and Coordination to End Homelessness State-wide," duplicated report (Richmond: Virginia Department of Housing and Community Development, May 2, 2017).

7. Virginia Homeless Outcomes Coordinating Council, "Homeless Outcomes Initiative 2010–2014: A Report to the Community," duplicated report (Richmond: Author, n.d.).

8. Homelessness Research Institute, National Alliance to End Homelessness, *The State of Homelessness in America* (Washington, DC: Author, 2016),10.

9. Point-in-time estimates furnished by Ms. Robertson.

10. Virginia Department of Veterans Services, "Governor McAuliffe Receives Award for Leadership in Functionally Ending Veteran Homelessness in Virginia," press release dated January 20, 2017. Retrieved online June 13, 2017.

CARLA D. HOLLOMAN, Social Worker
Public Servant of Children

Photo by Charles T. Goodsell

This second Public Well-Being essay possesses a focus that is wider than a policy area. Its context is a whole public profession, that of social work. Our subject is a senior social worker with much experience in domestic abuse and foster care in particular within an urban environment.

The social work profession in this country is another product of the Progressive Era and in large part the agitation of women. In 1889, Jane Addams and Ellen Gates Starr founded Hull House in Chicago, adopting the settlement house concept first tried in London as a place to aid and educate factory workers. In 1903, Lillian Wald and Florence Kelly discussed the notion of a government bureau devoted to reducing infant mortality. After obtaining the support of Theodore Roosevelt, the U.S. Children's Bureau was eventually established in 1912. Its first director was Julia Lathrop, and for the next half century the organization was almost exclusively headed and staffed by women.

Today, the U.S. social work profession is a fully developed enterprise. It embraces university undergraduate and graduate programs, research journals, accrediting organizations, granting institutions, social policy think tanks, and tens of thousands of state and local departments of social services—all of which is largely a female province of activity.[1]

At the same time, social work is not a stabilized or unified field but a diverse and dynamic one. It consists of many occupational categories: social caseworkers, entitlement eligibility workers, clinical therapists, career administrators, college teachers and scholars, public policy analysts, community organizers, and association lobbyists. Each group defines the work a bit differently. A big thematic gulf is between those who help individuals in trouble versus those preoccupied with the state of society. Members of the first group see their job as enabling the severely dispossessed to survive in the short run and reach their ultimate potential in the long run. That is the story told here. Those in the second group are devoted to improving conditions for the poor and ostracized elements of the population by structural social change. While the first group complains about inadequate budgets, the second bemoans oppressive systems.[2]

Mecklenberg County, North Carolina, first ventured into the public welfare arena in 1919. While women founded the field and do most of its work, this did not keep men from mostly managing it. The first superintendent of public welfare in Mecklenburg was a teacher in a boy's military school, Lucius Ranson. His tasks included monitoring school truancy, forming male recreation opportunities, receiving reports on the insane and destitute, and enforcing moral standards at movie theaters.

Eventually, the superintendent's office turned into what is known today as the Department of Social Services (DSS). From 1945 to 1972, the unit was led by Wallace Kuralt, a social work administrator who got his start in New Deal relief agencies. To illustrate the shift in professional norms during Kuralt's tenure, the agency's approach to human reproduction evolved from (1) mandatory sterilization to (2) condom distribution to (3) promotion of "the pill."

From 1994 to 2007, the department was led by Richard "Jake" Jacobsen. He did much to modernize it for contemporary needs. He established the state's first welfare-to-work program (he called it "Work First"), created a computerized information case management program that allows instant posting of client reports ("IZZY"), and nurtured a culture of treating clients as "customers" who deserve quick and courteous service.[3]

Mecklenburg County includes the city of Charlotte plus six small towns. The resulting catchment area of 500 square miles and a million people make this DSS the state's most important urban public welfare institution. At last word, the Department's workforce numbered approximately 1,200 personnel, of which 87 percent were female and 62 percent African American. They work in several buildings, the most important being the Kuralt Center, the agency's headquarters. The DSS operating budget is in the neighborhood of $200 million, of which about 40 percent comes from the county, 14 percent from the state, and 44 percent from Washington. This does not include approximately $1 billion in fiduciary funds that flow through the agency on their way to recipients in the form of cash assistance, SNAP credits (Food Stamps), Medicaid benefits, and other transfers.

The Department's director is appointed by the County Board of Commissioners and administratively she reports to the county manager. Line programs are organized in three divisions: Economic Services, which manages Work First, SNAP, Medicaid, and WIC; Adult Services, which handles investigation of elder abuse, operation of senior nutrition sites, and transportation of the elderly and disabled; and Youth and Family Services, which investigates child, family, and sexual abuse, and arranges for foster care and adoption. This last division is where our subject is employed.

Carla D. Holloman was born in Chapel Hill, North Carolina, and was raised in low-income housing by a single mother who worked at least two jobs at a time. Carla's father was absent from the household. Upon graduating from high school, she left home to attend college, the first one in her family to do so. In 2001, North Carolina Agricultural and Technical University in Greensboro granted her a BA degree with a major in psychology.

A year after graduation, Carla gave birth to a baby boy, whom she named David. Six weeks following David's birth, she married his father and moved with him to his hometown of Atlanta. To help make ends meet in the big city, she obtained a job in a private foster care agency, exposing her for the first time to social work. Although Carla found herself attracted to helping children, the work was unsatisfying and the pay low. Unfortunately, the marriage did not work out and ended in divorce.

At this juncture in her life, Carla felt she had reached a crossroads. A bold step was needed to reset her life journey. Yet the prospects for doing so were not bright. She was 25 years old, newly divorced, a single parent, and had no salaried job or prospects of getting one. With trepidation yet determination, Ms. Holloman decided to aim for a career in professional social work and obtain the educational background necessary to do so. A scholarship for graduate work in the field came to her attention, for which she applied. A Child Welfare Education Collaborative grant was awarded that Carla used to enter a Master of Social Work (MSW) program sponsored jointly by her alma mater A&T and the University of North Carolina-Greensboro, where she enrolled. Looking back, Carla will never forget the day she set out to return to her native state for this new start—armed, as she recalls, "with $700 and a prayer."

For the next two years in graduate school, Carla carried a full load of courses while holding three part-time jobs to supplement her stipend. One of these positions was at the Alamance County Department of Social Services in Burlington, North Carolina, 20 miles from campus. Her position there was that of child protective services investigator; this led to 17 months of being on duty on an as-needed basis as an innocent newcomer to the dangerous business of entering homes to check on abuse and neglect complaints.

Upon graduating with the MSW in 2007, Ms. Holloman assumed her first full-time social work job right there in Greensboro, at the Guilford County Department of Social Services. Her position in the agency was again that of child protective services investigator. In addition to family abuse cases, she investigated allegations of irregularity at daycare centers and group homes, bringing the young social worker in touch again with the private-sector side of her field as experienced in Atlanta.

After nearly four years at Guilford, Carla was delighted to obtain a position in the state's largest DSS department in Mecklenburg County. She moved with little David to the City of Charlotte in January 2011. In light of her background, Carla was assigned to Mecklenburg's Division of Youth and Family Services, where she has remained since.

At this writing, Ms. Holloman holds the rank of senior social worker. Her job title is that of permanency planning social worker, a phrase that refers to the task of working out care scenarios for children who have, for their own safety, been removed by the department from the custody of their biological parents or formal caregivers. The options available in these scenarios are (1) enrollment in rehabilitative social services for parents followed by reunification with the family if possible, by far the preferred outcome; (2) temporary placement with foster parents while a determination is made as to whether reunification is possible; and (3) permanent adoption by a guardian or new family when no alternative course of action is available.

Within the division, Carla is a member of a five-person team dedicated to permanency planning. As such, she and her teammates are responsible for casework decisions during the fluid and critical period spanning options (1) and (2) above. Her team leader is Mr. David Fee, a DSS veteran with long experience in this area. Director of the Youth and Family division is Mr. Charles Bradley, who in turn reports to the Department's director, Ms. Peggy Eagan.

Over the course of the many job experiences just outlined, Carla underwent several inner transformations that shaped how she carries out her job today as a social worker in the Charlotte metro area. Each change moment has added to a growing accumulation of personal insights that she presently carries with her as she encounters the challenges of this demanding profession.

A realization achieved early on at Guilford is to watch out for one's own health and well-being. In a job in which one is simultaneously responsible for trying to make better the life of multiple desperate individuals, there is always the temptation to do more on a given day. After misjudging a few times the attention and energy she was devoting to clients versus to herself and David, Carla realized that to perform her job well a proper balance must be maintained between job and personal life.

Another epiphany-type moment occurred when one evening she and her boyfriend dropped in for kicks at a local "gentlemen's club." To Carla's astonishment, one of the dancers performing was a young woman who had been a sexually abused girl she had previously mentored and monitored in a group setting. As the shock sank in, Carla realized fully for the first time how important it is for young women to develop a healthy and constructive self-image. The task is especially difficult for workers in the sex industry who, in the vast majority of cases, live subconsciously as "wounded little girls" seeking male approval. This incident has remained in her mind since as she counsels girls.

Another insight was acquired when Carla self-examined her own parenting skills and attitudes. In elementary school, her son David acted out excessively to the extent of becoming a disturbance in the classroom. When his teachers introduced to Carla the possibility that he was suffering from ADHD (attention deficit hyperactivity disorder), Carla loudly refused to accept this explanation and instead attributed it to a high level of intelligence combined with boredom in the classroom. As time went on, however, she relaxed her defensiveness, acknowledged the teachers were probably right, and agreed to initiating professional help. What this experience taught was that when welfare parents—beset anyway by myriad sources of stress—rant and rave over their children's conduct, she could truly appreciate their state of mind. Ever since, she has been able to defuse the frustration felt by clients over their kids' behavior by joking about and sharing her own experience in this regard.

A fourth self-discovery occurred for Carla when she witnessed instances where children under agency care met violent death. She discovered far deeper than at a mere intellectual level that social work is not only about human uplift but also about human tragedy. One time she had to attend the funeral of an abused boy so as to have an opportunity to question his mother about endangering her surviving children. In another case, a 12-year-old girl she was working with hanged herself without warning. Once when the agency did not act quickly enough to remove a 6-year-old little girl from the home of an abusive family, she was later found beaten and starved to death. This last incident caused the entire department to pause and reflect on its duty.

A final inner transformation occurred during an episode of personal depression that set in soon after Ms. Holloman's arrival in Mecklenburg. Despite getting this good job with a promising future in a prestigous agency, she felt deep down something was missing. Gradually, she saw herself entering "a dark place" in which she was not relating well to others and could not figure out what was wrong. She talked to her beloved grandmother about it and was told to "give birth to your pain," and when it is outside of you, "give it a name."

This piece of wisdom gave Carla the key to unlocking her dark place. When the "it" pain was named, it turned out to be bottled-up hostile feelings associated with family relationships experienced in her childhood. Uncovering this hidden hurt was aided by reading a book that advises adults to reconnect with their early roots.[4] In due course, Carla began to discuss openly with family members what she was going through, and gradually, the depression lifted as she brought to the surface what had been bothering her. The resulting sense of liberation again enabled Carla to relate personally to troubled clients and help them understand themselves.

At this point in the essay we turn to the program content of Ms. Holloman's work. As we have seen, her career has centered on two interconnected social work functions: child protection investigation and foster care planning. Speaking of the first, in Mecklenburg County calls alleging abuse or neglect of children and adults are received in a specially equipped room in what is known as the department's Charlotte East Building. It is staffed by trained intake personnel on a 24/365 basis with one crew scheduled for day duty and another for night. Calls come in on a dedicated abuse hotline number, 704-336-CARE. The calls typically originate from family members, relatives, neighbors, police officers, hospital staff, or school personnel. The nature and circumstance of the activity are noted by the operator, and an intake supervisor determines whether the indicated behavior legally constitutes abuse.[5] If so, and if violent harm or serious neglect has occurred or is likely to happen soon, an investigator is assigned the case who immediately jumps in a county car and departs for the site. Not all reports describe an imminent emergency, and these are followed up later. In a typical year, 500 to 800 adult abuse calls are received by the agency and as many as 12,000 for child abuse; some 2,000 open cases are continuously pending.[6]

As we have seen, Ms. Holloman investigated child abuse or neglect cases in Alamance and Guilford Counties. In so doing, she developed a series of prudent steps she regularly took before proceeding. She would always inform an associate in the office where she was going and when she expected to return. If information is known about weapons in the house or of a parent with a violent criminal record, the police are either asked to be on alert or parked at the address. Then, after knocking on the door and entering the dwelling, Carla had the habit of standing near the open portal until conditions were established as safe. Her practice with respect to opening conversations was not to act as someone in authority looking for guilty parties, but as a caring professional who has come to gather information. She would then attempt to interview every person present in the house, including children and relatives.

Throughout the visit, the prime objective is to be assured of the child's or adult's current safety. A secondary aim is to discuss with the parents or other caregivers the services that are available to stabilize the situation, such as keeping a responsible relative always present, undergoing detoxification, or entering a counseling program. Since domestic abusers commonly manipulate others and act impulsively, Carla always kept alert to sudden acts of rage. She learned of this harsh reality one day early in her career when an angry father suddenly threatened to hit her. Her supervisor stepped between them and ordered him to back off or expect police arrest, which he did. The quick action became a model to remember for the young investigator.

Ms. Holloman points out that childhood sexual abuse specifically has cursed the lives of approximately one out of three women and one out of five men. Investigating this horrendous crime requires sensitivity and special skills. Almost always the scars are not physical but psychological and hence hidden from view.

Detecting these in children is an especially delicate matter. One device she often used was to gauge the content of the child's sex vocabulary. If a boy does not know the word *penis* or the girl *vagina* but only euphemistic nicknames, this practice may have been encouraged by a pedophile. If these verbal substitutes are then used to describe sexual activities not normally known about at that child's age level, the evidence is strong that something is wrong.

If the responsible social worker, department superiors, and the division attorney agree that it necessary to remove a child from a home, a court order is normally required. In hearing the case, the judge makes certain that all alternative solutions have been pursued to no avail and removal remains the only option. If an emergency is sensed that no time is available for a court hearing, the agency is permitted to exercise on its own up to 12 hours of mandatory custody. The act of removing a child from his or her parents is multilayered and emotional for all involved; even though doing so may not produce the Hollywood dramatics one might expect, the day on which it happens is forever etched in the minds of all persons involved.

Once custody is obtained, within 30 to 45 days the department must prepare for and secure court approval for a plan to care for the child. This is where the permanency planning activity in which Ms. Holloman is currently engaged comes into play. If possible, the plan will aim to return the child to his or her parents after a prescribed regime of social services and/or therapeutic rehabilitation. During this period the boy or girl is placed in the care of a guardian or foster family. At a later time, court approval for experimental parental recontact may be attempted. This may be done by temporary home visits with a relative present or ones arranged outside the home, such as supervised DSS play rooms for infants and toddlers.

If all these corrective steps fail, the only way out short of indefinite foster care (very seldom used) is adoption, by either a recruited family or guardian. Such a step is considered sufficiently serious that it requires a formal trial in domestic court. With all parties present with their attorneys, the caseworker and other involved parties testify with respect to the circumstances and evidence brought forward by the state in support of a permanent termination and transfer of parental rights.

It is the task of arranging and monitoring of foster care that occupies most of the work time of Carla and her permanency planning teammates. A preliminary matter of vital importance is to recruit suitable foster parents and match them well with individual foster children. Problems to look out for are parental candidates that seem too motivated by the amount of monetary care payments provided and those who believe the answer to all interpersonal domestic disagreements is solemn prayer absent all professional intervention. A number of other factors must be considered as well, such as the relative ages of the foster child and adults and how much medical care or daily supervision is necessary. Often, persons who have themselves grown up in foster family care are ideal.

At this writing, Carla's foster caseload is thirteen boys and girls. She calls them "her babies" and loves to joke with them, be cheerful and upbeat, and talk to them about life's obstacles, while at the same time inspiring hope. She visits each one individually and regularly in the foster home setting in order to check household conditions and inquire how things are going. On other occasions, she may arrange meetings with the child alone at school or elsewhere in the community.

Each case is unique. The child–family match may work out well and the foster experience may be very positive. Or it may generate chronic and bitter conflict that requires termination of the arrangement and an alternative placement. A common reason for the latter is when lingering loyalty persists on the part of the girl or boy to biological parents. Indeed, the best outcome possible in any foster situation is reuniting the child with her or his original family. To maximize chances for such a conclusion, Carla considers an integral part of her job to be monitoring the progress of each case carefully. This includes attempting to understand the history and dynamics of the dysfunctional family involved and how to break through its cycle of destructive relationships. In some instances, she is able to achieve her goal within a few months, while in others the process of rehabilitation and encouragement goes on for years or fails outright. Her most rewarding moment is when one of her "babies" safely returns home and stays there.

Looking at Ms. Holloman's career as a totality, we can see that its dominant theme is the care of troubled children. Back when preparing for her "$700 and a prayer" leap, she had already worked with youngsters in a private agency but had not yet set her mind in that direction. However, the scholarship that enabled her to take the leap specifically dealt with this occupational decision, and the fit turned out to be perfect. In the succeeding years of her career in government—in three county departments of social services—her principal area of activity was child protection.

In the process of doing this very important work, Ms. Holloman herself grew as a person and as a professional. She states openly that she loves social work and wants to remain in Mecklenburg County for the rest of her career. Moreover, she hopes eventually to advance to positions of leadership in the organization that would enable her to amplify the effects of what she has acquired by transferring her skills and insights to the next generation of child welfare workers. Nothing would satisfy her more than to promote the kind of social work she would have wanted but did not get for her family back in Chapel Hill when she was young. Her calling springs from deep within.

NOTES

1. Arthur E. Fink, Jane H. Pfouts, and Andrew W. Dobelstein, *The Field of Social Work* (Beverly Hills, CA: Sage, 1985), Ch. 1. See also Frederic G. Reamer, ed., *The Foundations of Social Work Knowledge* (New York: Columbia University Press, 1994), Ch. 1 and Ch. 2. Interestingly enough, even the first recorded victim of child abuse was female. In 1874, a girl named Mary Ellen needed protection, but the only laws available to shield her had to do with the abuse of animals, a point that spurred new legislation.

2. Lena Dominelli, *Social Work: Theory and Practice for a Changing Profession* (Cambridge, UK: Polity Press, 2004).

3. Goodsell, *Mission Mystique: Belief Systems in Public Agencies* (Washington, DC: CQ Press, 2011), 141–146. When in his New Deal days, Kuralt drove around North Carolina to inspect welfare offices, and he often took his son Charles with him. This offspring became the Charles Kuralt that originated the "On the Road" segment still seen on the *CBS Evening News*.

4. Monica McGoldrick, *You Can Go Home Again: Reconnecting with Your Family* (New York: W.W. Norton, 1995).

5. Legal definitions vary by state. In federal law, child abuse and neglect is defined as "physical or mental injury, sexual abuse or exploitation, negligent treatment, or maltreatment of a child by a person who is responsible for the child's welfare, under circumstances which indicate that the child's health or welfare is harmed or threatened thereby." Susan J. Wells, "Child Abuse and Neglect Overview," *Encyclopedia of Social Work*, 19th ed. (Washington, DC: National Association of Social Workers, 1995), 346–353 at 347. A feature of North Carolina abuse law is that anyone over the age of 18 is mandated to report suspected instances of abuse or neglect.

6. Goodsell, *Mission Mystique*, 150, 152.

JEFFREY B. RICHARDSON, County Manager
Much Responsibility Closely Watched

Photo by Charles T. Goodsell

This third essay in the realm of Public Well-Being is focused like a wide-angle lens. The responsibilities of the chief executive of an entire county government cover a great deal of ground. The same can be said for the field of public administration itself; thus, this feature seems appropriate for the final contribution to a set of essays that sound a fanfare for the common bureaucrat.

Jeffrey Richardson was born in Black Mountain, North Carolina, a town on the western side of the state 10 miles east of Asheville. His parents owned a Sears Roebuck catalog store through his growing-up years. During this time, young Jeff could not help but notice how his parents took pains to treat customers courteously and see to it their needs were met by prompt shipments from the company.

About the time Jeff began to attend college in Asheville, the store was sold, freeing his father from daily responsibilities. In an unexpected twist of fate, a short time later, the current city manager of Black Mountain suddenly left office. Members of the town council were stymied on a successor and asked the popular Mr. Richardson to take over, despite his lack of training in municipal management. Thus, while Jeff was being introduced to subjects like political science at the University of North Carolina-Asheville, his father was learning from scratch the ropes of public administration back in Black Mountain. When over the next four years Jeff came home for dinner, their separate learning curves intersected at the family table. Soon, the son was dreaming of becoming a city manager like his dad.

Upon graduating with a BA, Jeff took a big step to fulfill his dream by enrolling in the Master of Public Administration (MPA) program at the University of North Carolina School of Government in Chapel Hill. Manager Richardson had already beat him to it, having entered the same program on a part-time basis to make up for his lack of training. For a time father and son were sharing the same local government classes. Professor A. John Vogt's course in municipal financial management was one of their favorites.

Today, our subject recalls lessons learned from his father, such as the need to treat each complaining citizen with face-to-face empathy, just as he did in the Sears store. Another lesson was that when a member of the public takes the trouble personally to visit his city hall, it is automatically the most important event in that person's day. Mr. Richardson continued to serve as city manager of Black Mountain for twenty years and continues to this day to lend advice and support to his son.

In his MPA program, Jeff chose personnel management as a special emphasis over financial management or public works. He graduated in 1990, and after a year and a half working at the university, he landed a job with Cleveland County, North Carolina, as director of human resources. Named after a colonel in the Revolutionary War, the county is located on the South Carolina border between Charlotte and Hendersonville. With a population of 85,000 at the time, its economy depended heavily on the textile industry. Jeff took up residence in the county seat of Shelby. Much farmland and fifteen other towns and villages are scattered across the county's 468 square miles. With Shelby being only 50 miles or so from Black Mountain and 70 from Asheville, it was not far from home.

Jeff remained in this position for six years, gaining experience in hiring, retraining, and motivating a public workforce. Eager to try out a bigger jurisdiction, he applied for and obtained a comparable position in the city government of Asheville. In cooperation with community leaders, in the 1980s and 1990s this city had carried out a successful program of downtown revitalization. Integral to this effort was emergence of a local music scene plus a set of quality restaurants that made for an attractive tourist destination. Together with the nearby presence of the Biltmore Estate, Blue Ridge Parkway headquarters, and National Climate Data Center, its local economy had undergone a surge and become the focal point of a large metro area.

Jeff remained employed by Asheville for 16 years. After four years of heading the Department of Human Resources, he was advanced to the position of deputy city manager. In this position, he supervised the departments of Police, Fire, General Services, Human Resources, and Information Technology. He learned firsthand that every day is different at the top managerial rung of a large city.

However, after 13 years in this capacity, Jeff's goal became management of a city or county where he could gain experience recruiting new industry for economic development. Asheville's economy was, in his eyes, too dependent on the service industry that supports its needs as a travel-destination city. Since most people who work there live and shop in non-annexed suburbs, city government was capturing only a fifth of area property and sales tax receipts.

In light of this uncertainty, Jeff took notice when he heard that his former employer, Cleveland County, had lost its county manager and was recruiting a replacement. He talked at length with his wife and father, and in spite of going back rather than moving on being unusual in his profession, he applied for the job and got it. What attracted him was the fact that the economy of Cleveland County was no longer depending on textiles but moving forward to bring in new jobs. The county board and outgoing administration had formed an Economic Development Partnership with the State of North Carolina, City of Shelby, City of Kings Mountain, and certain key agencies. Together they successfully induced manufacturing corporations to locate plants in the county on the basis of proximity to Charlotte's airport and the county's central position between there and Asheville. The county's population had by this time left the 85,000 mark behind and was now approaching 100,000 residents.

Jeff Richardson assumed the position of Cleveland County manager on September 30, 2013. His office is located in a brick two-story county executive building at 311 East Marion Street. The manager's office is a pleasant but not opulent space on the second floor with a window facing the street. Adjacent are a conference room, workroom, and reception office containing the desk of Ms. April Crotts, Jeff's assistant. Although other employees are nearby when needed, during normal business hours she handles everything he needs.

A few steps away from the manager's office lies the formal meeting chamber of the County Board of Commissioners. It is a large room dominated by a raised wooden dais extending across the width of the far end. Commissioners seated behind it face slightly downward to rows of comfortable audience seats. Exhibited on the wall behind the dais is a large carved version of the county seal. When in session, the dais seats five elected citizen commissioners plus room at the end for the manager, county clerk, and county attorney. Meetings are chaired by a commissioner elected annually by members to do so.

These physical arrangements are in keeping with the structure of Cleveland County government. Its head is the corporate body of part-time citizen commissioners elected for rotating four-year terms. The county manager is hired by the Commission and serves at its pleasure. This relationship is common to all 100 North Carolina counties.

However, the details of administrative organization below this level differ to some extent across the state. Bigger counties establish an Office of the County Manager that includes deputy and assistant county managers. Staff units such as finance director and county counsel are often incorporated, with line departments reporting upward in multiple hierarchical steps.

By contrast, Cleveland County's organization is quite flat. About the only intermediate reporting point between line activities and the county manager's personal office is Director of Community Services Kerri Melton, who supervises a cluster of departments and divisions. This gives Jeff a relatively large span of control to juggle. In the future, Jeff is planning to refine the organizational structure so that stronger checks and balances exist and management responsibilities are divided and streamlined under a new position classification system.

A measure of decentralization is present in most U.S. counties anyway because of multiple authorities serving the same citizenry. All North Carolina counties have separately elected sheriffs that perform police, jail, and court support functions. County boards of education operate the schools, and in Cleveland County the Board of Education has more employees than the county by a wide margin. Other independent entities are the Register of Deeds, District Attorney, and Clerk of Court, all of whom are elected. Local District and Superior Courts are under the jurisdiction of the state.

But County Manager Richardson is personally responsible for all of the rest. And this is not an insignificant amount of territory: the daily work of 860 full-time county employees and the expenditure of more than $130 million annually that funds thirteen departments and at least ten smaller units.

Even without competing authorities, complexities still arise. Jeff supervises law enforcement activities not covered by the sheriff but located in the same building with him, the Justice Center. These include a 911 Communications Center, an Emergency Medical Services (EMS) Department, and an Emergency Management Department that stocks emergency supplies and helps manage an emergency alarm system.

Two county buildings on South Post Road stand next to each other in a plot designated the County Health and Human Services campus. Its Social Services component operates a full range of welfare programs, including child abuse, foster care, emergency assistance, and food and nutrition programs. The second structure, recently under construction, houses the county Health Department, which offers child, school, and maternity health services; immunizations; family planning; and cancer screening. Both departments operate with their own citizen advisory boards.

Other Cleveland County agencies engage in economic development promotion, animal control, refuse recycling, soil and water conservation, building inspection, historic preservation, veterans' services, and tax collection. Two public libraries operate in towns around the county and a modern central landfill is managed to serve the greater area. Overhead staff agencies consist of the departments of Planning, Finance, Human Resources, Information Technology, and Maintenance.

Extensive collaborative activity makes the number of balls in the air for Jeff to juggle even greater. The Health Department collaborates with the nonprofit Alliance for Health to sponsor an annual Step One Challenge that urges citizens to take daily walks 10,000 steps long. In cooperation with the North Carolina Wildlife Resources Commission, a first-order shooting range for rifles, pistols, and archery has been in the works. A premier event venue known as the LeGrand Center in Shelby was constructed in partnership with Cleveland Community College and its Foundation, as well as the Cleveland County Public School System. However, it is now exclusively owned and operated by the county.

The collaborative work making the greatest impact on county life is the Cleveland County Economic Development Partnership. It has enabled the City of Shelby and Cleveland County to establish a co-owned Foothill Commerce Center, just west of Shelby. This industrial park is equipped with filled factory shell buildings and available flat pads of land connected to utilities. With the state's cooperation, safe financial incentives in the form of post-performance tax grants are available and have induced a wide and diverse mix of industry to come into the county.

Unlike the new-industry priority of the previous administration, Jeff's focus has grown in the past two years and is now centered on the need to have sufficient adequately skilled workers on hand as a sound reason to invest in Cleveland County. This policy objective is expressed as workforce readiness. A taskforce for this purpose has been instrumental in persuading Cleveland public schools to offer relevant college preparation courses and the local Cleveland Community College to conduct certificate programs in such areas as robotics and advanced machine control. By late 2016, the county had gained more than 300 new manufacturing jobs, and from 2012 to 2016 the unemployment rate declined from 10.6 percent to 5.6 percent.

So, we are discussing in this essay the manager of a mid-sized county in North Carolina who is under close watch by an elected citizen board while being responsible for a large, diverse and fragmented organizational domain. Moreover, he is doing it with an essentially flat but complex organizational structure in activities involving multiple other actors both public and private.

Yet despite these complications and responsibilities, Mr. Richardson has appeared to do well. He has balanced the budget each year with a substantial end-of-year surplus. County revenues have increased without raising taxes. A new sustainable county employee pay plan study is underway, and the county anticipates a multiyear modernized pay structure and new steps to reduce turnover. The county's bond rating has gone up during his tenure and a five-year capital improvement plan is being prepared. In 2015, a Certificate of Achievement in Financial Reporting was received from the Government Finance Officers Association.

With respect to outcomes for the citizenry, additional industry has been attracted to the county in light of the Economic Development Partnership. More and more building permits have been issued in recent years. The Public Health Building and Public Shooting Range have been completed. A small business loan program has been initiated to encourage investments by small-sized firms.

The Partnership is concerned not only about factories. A Strategic Plan goal has been set to develop further the county's strong but stable agricultural economy. As the county's economy continues to grow, more discussions are underway in the public and private sectors to heighten the county's "sense of place." An example is discussions on best practices for tearing down dilapidated buildings and beautifying Route 74, the county's major highway.

Jeff's successful work has been recognized outside Cleveland County. He was elected chair of the Western North Carolina City and County Managers Association. His reputation has reached the state's academic establishment in Chapel Hill, where he is regarded as one of North Carolina's best rising local government managers. On weekends, he regularly teaches classes as a fellow and adjunct professor at the UNC School of Government in Chapel Hill and is on its MPA Board of Directors.

What is our subject's secret? My guess is three things.

One is a gregarious, outgoing personality. Jeff speaks articulately with force and spontaneity. He can lead aggressively but at the same time listen humbly. He is good at both planning ahead and keeping track of details. The roles of persuader, mediator, and negotiator come naturally. Although not personally liked by all citizens, Jeff can deal comfortably with all manner of people in a variety of social situations, a trait probably learned from his father. He makes a point of visiting less settled portions of the county to keep in touch with its residents. Stimulated intellectually by his teaching trips to Chapel Hill, he is passionate about continuing education in order to keep thinking creatively.

A second factor is Jeff's efforts to build and strengthen the organization's culture. In the realm of cultural leadership, he has introduced a TRUE BLUE formulation that is used in training sessions. Its letters point to employee Talent, Role, Understanding, and Effort that make it possible for the organization to gain greater Belief, Loyalty, Unity, and Evolve (growth). The purpose of the exercise is to create additional organizational alignment between employee attitudes and public service principles so that when county citizens are treated better, those who serve them experience personal fulfillment.

Not long after Jeff arrived on the scene, the county entered into a partnership with the YMCA to develop and operate a physical wellness program for employees. It is called Cleveland Strong. Over time, however, participants got the idea that the word *Strong* could be extended from personal Strong wellness to organizational wellness. After two years of staff discussion, the idea blossomed into a major culture-building memory device: STRONG—S for service to the public; T for teamwork within the organization; R for the respect paid to others; O for opportunities to grow; N for networking to solve problems; and G for also getting physically healthy.

A third key is Mr. Richardson's relationship with his board. He sees his role as being able to earn the trust of the commissioners while at the same time helping them to function at a collective board level and accomplish as much as possible. He advises and thinks of implications of new policies but follows their policy guidance faithfully. At each session of the board (twice a month), several "actions" are formally voted upon and inscribed in the minutes as the official basis for a subsequent response. Each year, the board works out its own list of strategic goals that, for 2016–2017, fell into the categories of Community Education and Customer Service Outreach, Economic Development, Public Safety, and Fiscal Sustainability.

During formal meetings, Jeff always takes care from his side seat at the dais to possess a command of the facts that the board members can rely on as a basis of action. When policy issues raise questions in need of staff input, he is not above suggesting opportunities for temperance. When presenting himself a problem or proposal for the board's consideration, he offers options for resolution, not a single recommendation. When department heads present reports, they have been approved by him and are presented through him.

On all matters, the county manager assumes an attitude of being flexible and open to new ideas. He recognizes how each commissioner brings to the dais a different background and interests. Not infrequently, Jeff discusses matters with members individually but only with subsequent sharing the matter with the others. All board members are publically affiliated with one of the two major political parties, but the current membership does not engage in partisan debate. Most have been reelected to their four-year term and hence board stability generally reigns. One important detail is that prior to each regular 6 o'clock bimonthly meeting, they gather within Jeff's workroom for a hot meal.

In short, conditions of civility, open dialogue, reasoned argument, and mutual respect prevail in this quite remarkable face-to-face version of American municipal democracy. Too bad such conditions are not more common elsewhere in our democracy as a whole.

Postscript: Readers will be interested to know that as of November 2017, Mr. Richardson is the new county executive for Albemarle County in Virginia. Given what we have learned about his conduct and accomplishments in Cleveland County, we should not be surprised. We offer our congratulations to Jeff and congratulate that jurisdiction for acquiring as a leader such a fine common bureaucrat.

REVIEW AND CONCLUSIONS

I n my introductory comments to this book, I argued that research in the field of public administration should conduct more study "inside" individual public servants. In this book, I have tried to do that. Here at the book's conclusion we will stand back and ask what we have learned about these twelve common bureaucrats—as individual actors.

An initial point that occurs to me is that each of these twelve not only possesses an external reputation of being outstanding, the criterion by which I asked nominators to observe when proposing candidates, he or she harbors that realization, too, internally—they *know full well they are good.*

Adam Price realizes he is a valuable source to the intelligence community on international gun running—he gets calls from the highest federal agencies for help. Michael Bender cannot escape the realization that he is a true "comer" in the eyes of Richmond police officials; his successive promotions prove it. Stephanie Pechura is continuously trusted by her superiors at the Virginia Center for Behavioral Rehabilitation for handling tough, critical jobs, such as installing a wireless security system and supervising the facility's new construction.

Cindy Berndt will never admit it, but she is perfectly aware she is close to being indispensable as a storehouse of information on regulatory processes at the Virginia Department of Environment Quality. Karen Wilson has been endowed with such breadth of experience at the Kentucky Cabinet for Energy and Environment that she possesses the discretionary latitude and confidence of superiors to lead the way in thinking out the planning of the state's energy future. Howard Glenn may not be sufficiently recognized for his work by the Department of Public Utilities, but he knows full well that the water safety of Richmond is essentially in his hands.

Dan McKeague's Eastern Divide district being named the best in the south was probably not much of a surprise to him—although he will not take all the credit. Dan Riccio is totally conscious that the Livability program would not be what it is without him; the fact that he has been tapped for tourism director too speaks volumes. Keith Grupposo is on his way up within the Fairfax Court Services Unit, and without a scintilla of bragging, he admits the prominence of his role in the jail diversion program.

Kathy Robertson's highly tangible success in reducing homelessness in Virginia, that is, a drop of one third, cannot be and is not denied in her own mind. Carla Holloman was thrilled to be nominated for inclusion in this book by her department head, confirming her hard-sought sense of self-esteem. Jeff Richardson's success as manager in Cleveland County is amply evident, and his successful bid to become county executive officer of Albemarle County in Charlottesville confirms his advanced professional status.

A second general point is how many of our subjects were *influenced by their parents*. To Adam Price, his Kentucky State Trooper father was a model from childhood. He literally followed his footsteps into the ATF as an adult. Michael Bender's parents were both civil servants, and some sort of public service was always his aim as a young man. Howard Glenn's dad was the first and only African American fire chief of Henrico County, an achievement that has always remained in his mind as something to model. Daniel Riccio's father was a public safety officer at the Charleston navy yard, and joining the Charleston police department seemed the natural thing to do. His work there led to his being appointed to the Livability job. Keith Grupposo grew up in a family whose life centered on participation in team sports, and this atmosphere led to Keith's interest in the well-being of juveniles. Carla Holloman was raised by a single-parent mother under low-income conditions; a beloved grandmother helped her realize her personal potential. Jeff Richardson's father became a town manager in mid-life, and the two of them attended MPA graduate school together at the University of North Carolina; ever since, he has turned periodically to his dad for advice as he makes decisions with respect to his local government management career.

Higher education has been a big factor in these lives. The foundations of Stephanie Pechura's unusual career were laid in college internships. At the University of Arizona she had one in which she helped a mentally disturbed man at a public defender's office. At Virginia Commonwealth University, internships involved counseling at a Youth Emergency Shelter and providing mental health care in a VA hospital. Karen Wilson attended the University of Kentucky, where an unexpected internship in what later became the state government's Energy and Environment cabinet led eventually to her present job.

Dan McKeague first became interested in a career in the Forest Service when the district ranger of Ocala National Forest spoke at one of his classes at the University of Florida. A class Keith Grupposo was taking at Marymount College in Arlington County, Virginia, was visited by a corrections worker who talked about ex-offender reentry into society. To fulfill an internship requirement, he counseled adults under detention in Arlington and Fairfax Counties. The event that gave Carla Holloman the chance to start a new life at age 25 was receipt of a scholarship that allowed her to enroll in an MSW program in Greensboro, North Carolina. While there, she had her first experience investigating child abuse in nearby Burlington. Jeff Richardson not only obtained an MPA degree at the University of North Carolina, but when serving as manager in Cleveland County, he went there on weekends to teach in their School of Government.

With respect to how our twelve public servants see themselves and their jobs, a common characteristic that stands out in my mind is their *commitment to change*. They are not stand-pat conservatives or individuals afraid to advocate program change or being personally risk-averse to moving in new directions. Given how the popular stereotype of government bureaucracy envisions this mega-institution to be stale, inflexible, and status quo oriented, this point may seem remarkable. In elaboration of this point, I offer a brief comment on each of the twelve.

With respect to policy innovation, in his assignment at the ATF Phoenix field office, Adam Price approved the Wide Receiver operation with crucial restrictions later unfortunately breached in Fast and Furious. He parlayed his Miami and Phoenix experiences into becoming a top advisor on forming national policy on arms trafficking.

Michael Bender took the lead in bringing a working Crisis Intervention program to Richmond. He was instrumental in obtaining police department buy-in, introducing it to the police academy curriculum, developing cooperative ties to the Behavioral Health Authority, and establishing the Crisis Triage Center at Chippenham Hospital.

Stephanie Pechura has been a major force for introducing changes at the Virginia Center for Behavioral Rehabilitation that make life more tolerable for the men. These include cafeteria feeding with optional menus, the capacity for residents to obtain their own medical and dental appointments, and an expanded vocational training program.

Cindy Berndt's innovative contribution to environmental quality in Virginia has been not to make innovations herself but to enable others to make them. As each successive regulatory board was created, she was the person that managed its affairs. Then when the department itself issued a series of new rules, she kept them legal.

In Karen Wilson's case, she facilitates public policy change by serving as a long-term strategic thinker on how Kentucky can best balance its need for cheap energy for industrial use against trends away from use of fossil fuels. Earlier in her career, she introduced the Energy Star conservation program to the state.

Howard Glenn's creative accomplishment was to modernize stormwater management in Richmond. His exhaustive knowledge of the city's water infrastructure, his capacity to educate the public on the problem, and his ability to build a strong culture in his division's blue-collar workforce were indispensable to achieving this goal.

The underlying theme of Dan McKeague's leadership of the Forest Service Eastern District is keeping pace with ongoing changes in accepted forestry practices. This relates to prescribed burning, fire suppression, wildlife protection, safeguarding hillsides and streams, proper timber harvesting, and conservation of wilderness areas.

When the mayor of Charleston decided that the city needed a Livability program, he turned to Dan Riccio to make it work. By virtue of Dan's persistence, attention to detail, dependability, persuasiveness, and use of sensible application of rules, it has been an outstanding success. He has been an ideal innovation implementer.

Keith Grupposo has been a leader in introducing justified jail diversion practices to juvenile probation in Fairfax County. He has done this by insisting on objective screening methods, being reasoned rather than rabid in his advocacy, and stressing the need to bring families and the community into giving troubled youths a chance.

To enable homelessness reduction to succeed in Virginia, Kathy Robertson and her staff had to undertake a major institution-building campaign across the state. Working virtually from scratch, they established active Continuum-of-Care units in all major communities. Without this innovation activity, the program would have failed.

The innovation story for Carla Holloman is how she was able to expand her own social work capabilities by struggling through several early limitations. These transformations included steps toward her own self-fulfillment and work experiences that led to a deeper understanding of client problems and the harsh realities of social work.

While manager of Cleveland County, Jeff Richardson introduced many changes. Most were accomplished by collaboration within the community. Economic development, for example, was carried out not just by recruiting new industry but by promoting job readiness in cooperation with the high school and local college.

A final attribute that sticks out with respect to the twelve is *their personal courage*, whether physical or moral. One cannot help but be impressed with Adam Price's record of being a street cop in Clawson, that of Michael Bender doing so in Richmond, and that of Dan Riccio in Charleston. At times, physical danger is or was present for Stephanie Pechura from VCBR residents, Keith Grupposo from Juvenile Detention Center inmates, and Carla Holloman from abusers of children.

Cindy Berndt has the moral courage to say no to agency policy advocates, Karen Wilson the same to coal or environmental extremists, and Dan McKeague to demands from landowners, timber executives, and anti-pipeline fanatics. For their parts, Howard Glenn had the determination to insist on new taxes for stormwater construction, Kathy Robertson had the fortitude to abandon private sector salaries for lower state pay, and Jeff Richardson accepted the risks of abandoning a top position at glamorous Asheville for a little known county where he had once worked.

There you have it, readers: my fanfare for the common bureaucrat, scored for twelve instruments in behalf of the common good. These are not "case studies" in the sense of the neutral external observations of science. The profiles and videos constitute vicarious entrees into the personal lives and careers of actual human beings, reaching the nearest point to authentic understanding short of self-immersion by participant observation. Attaining these inside looks carries us to a new and deeper level of understanding and appreciation for bureaucracy in America—the hands, minds, and hearts of common bureaucrats who literally do the work of effective governance.

Hopefully these efforts will be supplemented in the future by other authors. Such depth of inquiry gives the field's scholarship a power of penetration it has seldom had, given our empirical dependence on superficial research sources like opinion surveys and remote "Big Data."

The method's nonrandomness, needed to express freely to the outside world the favorable outcomes of such study, is not a handicap. Preselecting excellence in subjects is instead an opportunity—a chance to counter the academy's traditional skepticism about bureaucracy and a way to attract young people to the noble profession of ground-level administration in a democratic society.

APPENDIX

Some Questions to Ponder from the Twelve Images and Essays

1. Reflect on how the following public administration topics come up among our subjects and point out comparisons that seem interesting.

Attitudes toward citizens	Leadership style
Basic values	Program success
Collaboration	Organizational culture
Dedication	Sense of mission

2. Which public servants among the twelve did you admire most? Explain why.

3. Did you come away from the book and videos with a different view of bureaucracy than you had previously?

4. What implications do the standards of bureaucratic conduct revealed here have for our democratic political system?

5. What do you think of the author's concept of "getting inside" these twelve public servants?

6. From a personal standpoint, has reading the book affected your thoughts about the future?

(If desired, share your opinions and ideas with the author via goodsell@vt.edu.)

INDEX

Patton, Governor Paul, 40
Pechura, Stephanie F., 22 (photo)
  biography of, 23–24
  career at VCBR, 24–25
  courage of, 110
  innovations by, 109
  internships, 24, 108
  pride in work, 28
  reputation, 107
  responsibilities, 25
Peck, Generra, 85
People Assisting the Homeless (PATH), 83
Permanency planning, 93
  adoption option, 96
  custody plan, 96
  experimental return, 96
  power to remove child, 96
  reunited family as aim, 97
Permanent Supportive Housing, 87
Peyton, Violet, 81
Phoenix, AZ, 7, 109
Piedmont Geriatric Hospital, 23
Pinchot, Gifford, 58, 59
Point-in-time homeless estimates, 81
Police enforcement action
  ATF special agents and, 4–5
  in Clawson, 4
  officer feelings regarding, xi
  in Miami, 5, 10
  in Richmond, 14–15
Police "Shoot, Don't Shoot" Force
    Simulator, 14
Post-performance corporate tax
    grants, 104
Pre-formed administrative decisions, 59
Prestonsburg, KY, 4
Price, Adam F., 2 (photo)
  biography of, 4–5
  career, 5–11
  Clawson experience, 4, 110
  dealing with prosecutors, 5
  evaluating agents, 6
  influence of father, 4, 108
  national and international consulting,
    8, 10, 109
  policy innovation, 119
  wide receiver program, 7, 109

Price, Philip, 4
Probation, history of, 73
Progressive Era, 57, 91
Prohibition Era, 3
Public shooting range, 104, 105

Quick Response Squad, 70

Ranson, Lucius, 91
Rapid rehousing, 87
Reagan, President Ronald, 9
Reducing family homelessness, 87
Region Eight of National Forest
    System, 60
Regulation as tool of governance, 31
Regulatory review steps in Virginia, 31
Residential Code Enforcement Teams, 69
Reston, VA, 75
Rhode Island, state of, 42
Riccio, Daniel M., 64 (photo)
  administrative style, 68–69
  biography of, 67, 108
  contribution to Charleston
  creates Livability division, 65
  enforcement values pursued, 68
  former police officer, 67, 110
  Livability director, 67
  reputation, 68, 107
  tourism director, 66
Richardson, Jeffrey B., 100 (photo)
  achievements at Cleveland County,
    104–106, 107, 110
  biography of, 101–102
  board relations, 106
  early position at Cleveland County, 101
  father as model, 101, 105, 108
  move to Albemarle County, 106, 108
  office used, 102
  personal traits, 105, 110
  teaching at UNC, 105, 108
  work in Asheville as deputy manager,
    102
Richmond, VA
  Bender's patrol experience here, 14–16,
    110
  Berndt's lifetime here, 32
  Glenn's work to keep city dry, 47–51, 109

ABOUT THE AUTHOR

Charles T. Goodsell was born and raised in Michigan and attended Kalamazoo College and, for graduate work, Harvard University. He served in the U.S. Army Counter Intelligence Corps in Berlin at the height of the Cold War. While interning at the U.S. Bureau of the Budget, he met and married a gorgeous Washington bureaucrat, Mary Elizabeth ("Liz") MacKintosh. They will soon celebrate their sixtieth wedding anniversary. Over 40 years, he taught mainly public administration and public policy at the University of Puerto Rico, Southern Illinois University, and Virginia Tech. At the last-named institution, he was a founding professor of the Center for Public Administration and Policy. Most of his publications concern administrative history, comparative administration, political economy, political interpretation of architecture, and government bureaucracy. He retired in 2002 and resides near Blacksburg, Virginia.